collections

Houghton
Mifflin
Harcourt

W9-ANE-808

Close Reader

GRADE 11

Program Consultants:

Kylene Beers

Martha Hougen

Carol Jago

William L. McBride

Erik Palmer

Lydia Stack

Copyright © by Houghton Mifflin Harcourt Publishing Company

All rights reserved. No part of this work may be reproduced or transmitted in any form or by any means, electronic or mechanical, including photocopying or recording, or by any information storage and retrieval system, without the prior written permission of the copyright owner unless such copying is expressly permitted by federal copyright law. Requests for permission to make copies of any part of the work should be addressed to Houghton Mifflin Harcourt Publishing Company, Attn: Contracts, Copyrights, and Licensing, 9400 Southpark Center Loop, Orlando, Florida 32819-8647.

Cover, Title Page Photo Credits: ©Michel Leynaud/Corbis

Printed in the U.S.A.

ISBN 978-0-544-09119-1

8 9 10   1421   22 21 20 19 18 17 16 15

4500534945   B C D E F G

If you have received these materials as examination copies free of charge, Houghton Mifflin Harcourt Publishing Company retains title to the materials and they may not be resold. Resale of examination copies is strictly prohibited.

Possession of this publication in print format does not entitle users to convert this publication, or any portion of it, into electronic format.

© Houghton Mifflin Harcourt Publishing Company

COLLECTION **1**

Coming to America

COLLECTION **2**

Building a Democracy

© Houghton Mifflin Harcourt Publishing Company • Image Credits: ©Dee Dee Yelverton/Flickr/Getty Images; ©Volanthevist/Flickr/Getty Images

fyi hmhfyi.com **Visit hmhfyi.com**
for current articles and
informational texts.

© Houghton Mifflin Harcourt Publishing Company • Image Credits: ©Max Oppenheim/Stone/Getty Images; ©Bettmann/Corbis

COLLECTION 5
An Age of Realism

COLLECTION 6
The Modern World

© Houghton Mifflin Harcourt Publishing Company • Image Credits: ©Nick Norman/National Geographic/Getty Images; ©Bek Shakirov/Images.com/Corbis

Visit hmhfyi.com
for current articles and
informational texts.

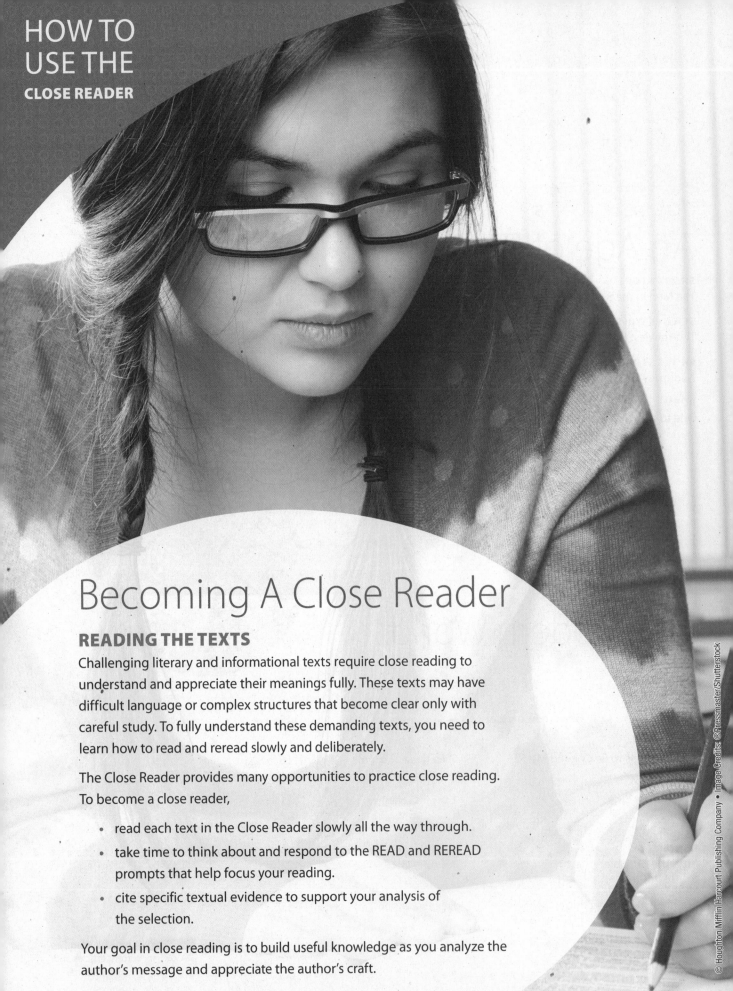

Becoming A Close Reader

READING THE TEXTS

Challenging literary and informational texts require close reading to understand and appreciate their meanings fully. These texts may have difficult language or complex structures that become clear only with careful study. To fully understand these demanding texts, you need to learn how to read and reread slowly and deliberately.

The Close Reader provides many opportunities to practice close reading. To become a close reader,

- read each text in the Close Reader slowly all the way through.
- take time to think about and respond to the READ and REREAD prompts that help focus your reading.
- cite specific textual evidence to support your analysis of the selection.

Your goal in close reading is to build useful knowledge as you analyze the author's message and appreciate the author's craft.

© Houghton Mifflin Harcourt Publishing Company • Image Credits: ©Pressmaster/Shutterstock

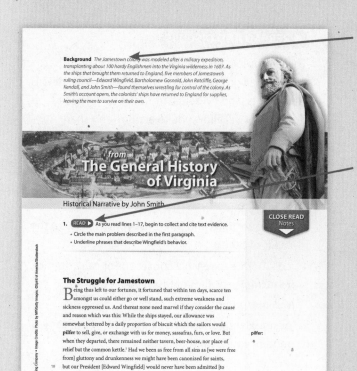

Background

This paragraph provides information about the text you are about to read. It helps you understand the context of the selection through additional information about the author, the subject, or the time period in which the text was written.

READ ▶

With practice, you can learn how to be a close reader. Questions and specific instructions at the beginning of the selection and on the bottom of the pages will guide your close reading of each text.

These questions and instructions

- refer to specific sections of the text.
- ask you to look for and mark up specific information in the text.
- prompt you to record inferences and text analysis in the side margins.
- help you begin to collect and cite text evidence.

Vocabulary

Critical vocabulary words appear in the margin throughout most selections. Consult a print or online dictionary to define the word on your own.

When you see a vocabulary word in the margin,

- write the definition in the margin.
- be sure your definition fits the context of the word as it is used in the text.
- check your definition by substituting it in place of the vocabulary word from the text. Your definition should make sense in the context of the selection.

◀ REREAD

To further guide your close reading, REREAD questions at the bottom of the page will

- ask you to focus on a close analysis of a smaller chunk of text.
- prompt you to analyze literary elements and devices, as well as the meaning and structure of informational text.
- help you go back into the text and "read between the lines" to uncover possible meanings and central ideas.

© Houghton Mifflin Harcourt Publishing Company

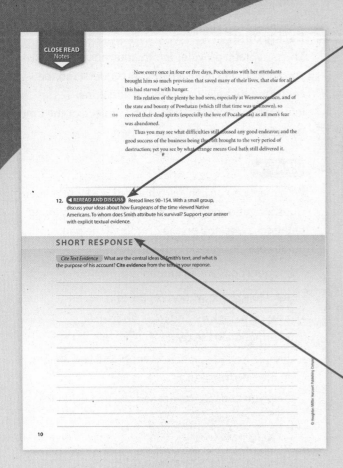

Now every once in four or five days, Pocahontas with her attendants brought him so much provision that saved many of their lives, that else for all this had starved with hunger.

His relation of the plenty he had seen, especially at Werowocomoco, and of the state and bounty of Powhatan (which till that time was unknown), so revived their dead spirits (especially the love of Pocahontas) as all men's fear was abandoned.

Thus you may see what difficulties still crossed any good endeavor; and the good success of the business being thus oft brought to the very period of destruction; yet you see by what strange means God hath still delivered it.

12. ◄ REREAD AND DISCUSS Reread lines 90–154. With a small group, discuss your ideas about how Europeans of the time viewed Native Americans. To whom does Smith attribute his survival? Support your answer with explicit textual evidence.

SHORT RESPONSE

Cite Text Evidence What are the central ideas of Smith's text, and what is the purpose of his account? **Cite evidence** from the text in your reponse.

© Houghton Mifflin Harcourt Publishing Company

10

◄ REREAD AND DISCUSS

These prompts encourage you to work with a partner or in a small group to discuss specific events, details, statements, and evidence from the text. These discussions will allow you to acquire and share knowledge about the texts you are reading.

As you engage in these discussions,

- be sure to cite specific text evidence in support of your statements.
- pose questions and integrate your ideas with the ideas of others.
- collaborate to reach a consensus or call attention to evidence that might have been missed or misinterpreted.
- acknowledge the views of others and be ready to modify your own thinking.

SHORT RESPONSE

At the end of each text, you will have an opportunity to sum up your thinking by completing a Short Response. The Short Response represents a place to convey some of the ideas you have developed through close reading of the text.

When you write your Short Response,

- review all of your margin notes and REREAD answers.
- circle or highlight evidence from your notes that supports your position or point of view.
- clearly state your point of view and support it with reasons.
- cite specific text evidence to support your reasons.

© Houghton Mifflin Harcourt Publishing Company

Coming to America

© Houghton Mifflin Harcourt Publishing Company © Image Credits: ©Dee Dee Yelverton/Flickr/Getty Images

COLLECTION **1**
Coming to America

"[In America] individuals of all nations are melted into a new race . . . whose labors . . . will one day cause great changes in the world."

—Michel-Guillaume Jean de Crèvecoeur

© Houghton Mifflin Harcourt Publishing Company ○ Image Credits: ©Dee Dee Yelverton/Flickr/Getty Images

Background *The Jamestown colony was modeled after a military expedition, transplanting about 100 hardy Englishmen into the Virginia wilderness in 1607. As the ships that brought them returned to England, five members of Jamestown's ruling council—Edward Wingfield, Bartholomew Gosnold, John Ratcliffe, George Kendall, and John Smith—found themselves wrestling for control of the colony. As Smith's account opens, the colonists' ships have returned to England for supplies, leaving the men to survive on their own.*

from The General History of Virginia

Historical Narrative by John Smith

CLOSE READ
Notes

1. **READD ▶** As you read lines 1–17, begin to collect and cite text evidence.

   • Circle the main problem described in the first paragraph.
   • Underline phrases that describe Wingfield's behavior.

The Struggle for Jamestown

Being thus left to our fortunes, it fortuned that within ten days, scarce ten amongst us could either go or well stand, such extreme weakness and sickness oppressed us. And thereat none need marvel if they consider the cause and reason which was this: While the ships stayed, our allowance was somewhat bettered by a daily proportion of biscuit which the sailors would **pilfer** to sell, give, or exchange with us for money, sassafras, furs, or love. But when they departed, there remained neither tavern, beer-house, nor place of relief but the common kettle.[1] Had we been as free from all sins as [we were free from] gluttony and drunkenness we might have been canonized for saints, but our President [Edward Wingfield] would never have been admitted [to sainthood] for engrossing to his private,[2] oatmeal, sack,[3] oil, aqua vitae,[4] beef,

pilfer:

10

---

[1] **common kettle:** food that was available to everyone.
[2] **engrossing to his private:** taking for his private use.
[3] **sack:** wine.
[4] **aqua vitae:** brandy.

© Houghton Mifflin Harcourt Publishing Company • Image Credits: Photo by MPI/Getty Images; ©Spirit of America/Shutterstock eggs, or what not but the kettle; that indeed he allowed equally to be distributed, and that was half a pint of wheat and as much barley boiled with water for a man a day, and this, having fried some twenty-six weeks in the ship's hold, contained as many worms as grains so that we might truly call it rather so much bran than corn; our drink was water, our lodgings castles in the air.

With this lodging and diet, our extreme toil in bearing and planting palisades[5] so strained and bruised us and our continual labor in the extremity
20 of the heat had so weakened us, as were cause sufficient to have made us as miserable in our native country or any other place in the world.

From May to September, those that escaped lived upon sturgeon and sea crabs. Fifty in this time we buried; the rest seeing the President's projects to escape these miseries in our pinnace[6] by flight (who all this time had neither felt want nor sickness) so moved our dead spirits as we deposed him and established Ratcliffe in his place (Gosnold being dead), Kendall deposed. Smith newly recovered, Martin and Ratcliffe were by his care preserved and relieved, and the most of the soldiers recovered with the skillful diligence of Master Thomas Wotton our surgeon general.

30 But now was all our provisions spent, the sturgeon gone, all helps abandoned, each hour expecting the fury of the savages, when God, the patron of all good endeavors, in that desperate extremity so changed the hearts of the savages that they brought such plenty of their fruits and provision as no man wanted.

industry:

The new President [Ratcliffe] and Martin, being little beloved, of weak judgment in dangers, and less **industry** in peace, committed the managing of all things abroad to Captain Smith, who, by his own example, good words, and fair promises, set some to mow, others to bind thatch, some to build houses, others to thatch them, himself always bearing the greatest task for his own
40 share, so that in short time he provided most of them lodgings, neglecting any for himself. . . .

---

[5] **palisades:** walls made of tall, pointed wooden stakes.
[6] **pinnace:** a small sailing ship.

2. **◀ REREAD** Reread lines 1–17. In the side margin, explain the central idea of this paragraph.

3. **READ ▶** Read lines 18–41. Underline text where Smith refers to himself.

4. **◀ REREAD** Reread lines 30–41. In the margin, explain why you think Smith refers to himself in the third person.

© Houghton Mifflin Harcourt Publishing Company

> *But now was all our provisions spent, the sturgeon gone, all helps abandoned, each hour expecting the fury of the savages . . .*

A Surprise Attack

Smith, perceiving (notwithstanding their late misery) not any regarded but from hand to mouth, (the company being well recovered) caused the pinnace to be provided with things fitting to get provision for the year following, but in the **interim** he made three or four journeys and discovered the people of Chickahominy,[7] yet what he carefully provided the rest carelessly spent.

Wingfield and Kendall, living in disgrace strengthened themselves with the sailors and other confederates to regain their former credit and authority,
50 or at least such means aboard the pinnace (being fitted to sail as Smith had appointed for trade), to alter her course and to go for England.

Smith, unexpectedly returning, had the plot discovered to him, much trouble he had to prevent it, till with the store of saker[8] and musket shot he forced them [to] stay or sink in the river: which action cost the life of Captain Kendall.[9]

These brawls are so disgustful, as some will say they are better forgotten, yet all men of good judgment will conclude it were better their **baseness** should be manifest to the world, than the business bear the scorn and shame of their excused disorders.

interim:

baseness:

---

[7] **Chickahominy:** a river in Virginia.
[8] **saker:** canon shot.
[9] **Captain Kendall:** Kendall was executed for mutiny in 1607.

---

5. **READD** ▷ As you read lines 42–62, continue to cite textual evidence. Paraphrase Wingfield and Kendall's plan in the margin on the next page. Explain what Smith does upon hearing about it.

© Houghton Mifflin Harcourt Publishing Company • Image Credits: ©Spirit of America/Shutterstock

60   The President and Captain Archer[10] not long after intended also to have abandoned the country, which project also was curbed and suppressed by Smith.

The Spaniard never more greedily desired gold than he [Smith] victual,[11] nor his soldiers more to abandon the country than he to keep it. But [he found] plenty of corn in the river of Chickahominy, where hundreds of savages in divers places stood with baskets expecting his coming. And now the winter approaching, the rivers became so covered with swans, geese, ducks, and cranes that we daily feasted with good bread, Virginia peas, pumpkins, and putchamins,[12] fish, fowl, and divers sort of wild beasts as fast as we could eat

70   them, so that none of our tuftaffety humorists[13] desired to go for England.

But our comedies never endured long without a tragedy, some idle exceptions being muttered against Captain Smith for not discovering the head of Chickahominy river and [he being] taxed by the Council to be too slow in so worthy an attempt. The next voyage he proceeded so far that with much labor by cutting of trees asunder he made his passage, but when his barge could pass no farther, he left her in a broad bay of danger of shot, commanding none should go ashore till his return, himself with two English and two savages went up higher in a canoe, but he was not long absent but his men went ashore, whose want of government gave both occasion and opportunity to the savages

80   to surprise one George Cassen whom they slew and much failed not to have cut off the boat and all the rest.

Smith little dreaming of that accident, being got to the marshes at the river's head twenty miles in the desert,[14] had his two men [Robinson and Emry] slain (as is supposed) sleeping by the canoe, while himself by fowling[15] sought

---

[10] **Captain Archer:** Gabriel Archer had abandoned the colony and then returned. He did not support Smith.

[11] **victual:** food.

[12] **putchamins:** persimmons.

[13] **tuftaffety humorists:** unreliable lace-wearers.

[14] **desert:** wilderness.

[15] **fowling:** hunting for birds.

---

6. **◀ REREAD AND DISCUSS**   Reread lines 42–62. With a small group, discuss the extent to which Smith's account seems credible. To what extent is this a factual narrative?

7. **READ ▶**   As you read lines 63–89, continue to cite textual evidence.

   • Underline the details that make Smith seem like a hero.

   • In the margin, explain the Council's complaint against Smith (lines 71–74).

© Houghton Mifflin Harcourt Publishing Company

them victual, who finding he was beset with 200 savages, two of them he slew, still defending himself with the aid of the savage his guide, whom he bound to his arms with his garters[16] and used him as a buckler,[17] yet he was shot in his thigh a little, and had many arrows that stuck in his clothes but no great hurt, till at last they took him prisoner. . . .

At Powhatan's Court

90   At last they brought him to Werowocomoco, where was Powhatan, their Emperor. Here more than two hundred of those grim courtiers stood wondering at him, as [if] he had been a monster, till Powhatan and his train had put themselves in their greatest braveries.[18] Before a fire upon a seat like a bedstead, he sat covered with a great robe made of raccoon skins and all the tails hanging by. On either hand did sit a young wench of sixteen or eighteen years and along on each side [of] the house, two rows of men and behind them as many women, with all their heads and shoulders painted red, many of their heads bedecked with the white down of birds, but every one with something, and a great chain of white beads around their necks.

---

[16] **garters:** shirtlaces.
[17] **buckler:** shield.
[18] **braveries:** clothes.

8. ◀ REREAD   Reread lines 63–89. What explanations does Smith give for the loss of men, and his own capture? Why does he include these explanations? Support your answer with textual evidence.

_____

_____

_____

_____

_____

9. READ ▶   As you read lines 90–135, continue to cite textual evidence.

• Underline language Smith uses to describe Powhatan.

• In the margin, explain what happens in lines 100–112.

© Houghton Mifflin Harcourt Publishing Company

100　At his entrance before the King, all the people gave a great shout. The
Queen of Appomattoc[19] was appointed to bring him water to wash his hands,
and another brought him a bunch of feathers, instead of a towel, to dry them;
having feasted him after their best barbarous manner they could, a long
consultation was held, but the conclusion was, two great stones were brought
before Powhatan; then as many as could, laid hands on him, dragged him to
them, and thereon laid his head and being ready with their clubs to beat out his
brains, Pocahontas, the King's dearest daughter, when no entreaty could
prevail, got his head in her arms and laid her own upon his to save him from
death, whereat the Emperor was contended he should live to make him

110　hatchets, and her bells, beads, and copper, for they thought him as well of all
occupations as themselves. For the King himself will make his own robes,
shoes, bows, arrows, pots; plant, hunt, or do anything so well as the rest.

　　Two days after, Powhatan, having disguised himself in the most fearfulest
manner he could, caused Captain Smith to be brought forth to a great house in
the woods and there upon a mat by the fire to be left alone. Not long after, from
behind a mat that divided the house, was made the most dolefulest noise he
ever heard; then Powhatan more like a devil than a man, with some two
hundred more as black as himself, came unto him and told him now that they
were friends, and presently he should go to Jamestown to send him two great

120　guns and a grindstone for which he would give him the country of
Capahowasic and forever esteem him as his son Nantaquoud.

　　So to Jamestown with twelve guides Powhatan sent him. That night they
quartered in the woods, he still expecting (as he had done all this long time of
his imprisonment) every hour to be put to one death or other, for all their
feasting. But almighty God (by His divine providence) had **mollified** the hearts
of those stern barbarians with compassion. The next morning betimes they
came to the fort, where Smith having used the savages with what kindness he
could, he showed Rawhunt, Powhatan's trusty servant, two demi-culverins[20]
and a millstone to carry [to] Powhatan; they found them somewhat too heavy,

130　but when they did see him discharge them, being loaded with stones, among
the boughs of a great tree loaded with icicles, the ice and branches came so
tumbling down that the poor savages ran away half dead with fear. But at last
we regained some conference with them and gave them such toys and sent
to Powhatan, his women, and children such presents as gave them in general
full content.

mollified:

_____
[19] **Appomattoc:** a nearby village.
[20] **demi-culverins:** large cannons.

 © Houghton Mifflin Harcourt Publishing Company

Pocahontas appeals to Powhatan to spare John Smith.

Now in Jamestown they were all combustion, the strongest preparing once more to run away with the pinnace; which, with the hazard of his life, with saker falcon and musket shot, Smith forced now the third time to stay or sink.

140   Some, no better than they should be, had plotted with the President the next day to have him put to death by the Levitical law,[21] for the lives of Robinson and Emry; pretending the fault was his that had led them to their ends; but he quickly took such order with such lawyers that he laid them by the heels[22] till he sent some of them prisoners for England.

---

[21] **Levitical law:** laws, ascribed to Moses, from the Book of Leviticus in the Old Testament.
[22] **laid them by the heels:** put them in prison.

---

10.   ◀ **REREAD AND DISCUSS**   Reread lines 90–135. With a small group, discuss why Smith included an account of his time with Powhatan.

11.   **READ** ▶   As you read lines 136–154, continue to cite textual evidence.

- Underline language that hints at Smith's attitude towards the "strongest" in Jamestown.
- In the margin, explain how Pocahontas again helped Smith.

 © Houghton Mifflin Harcourt Publishing Company • Image Credits: © North Wind Picture Archives/Alamy

Now every once in four or five days, Pocahontas with her attendants brought him so much provision that saved many of their lives, that else for all this had starved with hunger.

His relation of the plenty he had seen, especially at Werowocomoco, and of the state and bounty of Powhatan (which till that time was unknown), so
150   revived their dead spirits (especially the love of Pocahontas) as all men's fear was abandoned.

Thus you may see what difficulties still crossed any good endeavor; and the good success of the business being thus oft brought to the very period of destruction; yet you see by what strange means God hath still delivered it.

12. ◀ REREAD AND DISCUSS Reread lines 90–154. With a small group, discuss your ideas about how Europeans of the time viewed Native Americans. To whom does Smith attribute his survival? Support your answer with explicit textual evidence.

SHORT RESPONSE

Cite Text Evidence What are the central ideas of Smith's text, and what is the purpose of his account? **Cite evidence** from the text in your response.

_____

_____

_____

_____

_____

_____

_____

_____

_____

_____

© Houghton Mifflin Harcourt Publishing Company

Background *Although her mother wanted her to be a neurosurgeon and a concert pianist,* **Amy Tan** *found her own road to success by becoming a writer. Her first novel,* The Joy Luck Club, *is a collection of related stories told by four mothers and four daughters and was later turned into a film. Tan was born in Oakland, California, two and a half years after her parents fled China's Communist revolution and settled in the United States. As the daughter of immigrant parents, Tan says she grew up with two Englishes—American English and Chinese English.*

Mother Tongue

Essay by Amy Tan

CLOSE READ
Notes

1. **READ ▷** As you read lines 1–30, begin to collect and cite text evidence.

   • Underline text Tan uses that explains what Tan is not.
   • Circle words that explain how Tan describes herself.
   • In the margin, make a running list of the types of English Tan describes and how she describes them.

I am not a scholar of English or literature. I cannot give you much more than personal opinions on the English language and its variations in this country or others.

   I am a writer. And by that definition, I am someone who has always loved language. I am fascinated by language in daily life. I spend a great deal of my time thinking about the power of language—the way it can evoke an emotion, a visual image, a complex idea, or a simple truth. Language is the tool of my trade. And I use them all—all the Englishes I grew up with.

   Recently, I was made keenly aware of the different Englishes I do use. I was
10 giving a talk to a large group of people, the same talk I had already given to half a dozen other groups. The talk was about my writing, my life, and my book *The Joy Luck Club*, and it was going along well enough, until I remembered one major difference that made the whole talk sound wrong. My mother was in the room. And it was perhaps the first time she had heard me give a lengthy speech, using the kind of English I have never used with her. I was saying things like "the intersection of memory and imagination" and "There is an aspect of my fiction that relates to thus-and-thus"—a speech filled with

© Houghton Mifflin Harcourt Publishing Company • Image Credits: ©Cori Wells Braun/Corbis; ©Monkey Business Images/Shutterstock

carefully wrought grammatical phrases, burdened, it suddenly seemed to me,
with nominalized[1] forms, past perfect tenses, conditional phrases, forms of
20 standard English that I had learned in school and through books, the forms of
English I did not use at home with my mother.

Just last week, as I was walking down the street with her, I again found
myself conscious of the English I was using, the English I do use with her. We
were talking about the price of new and used furniture, and I heard myself
saying this: "Not waste money that way." My husband was with us as well, and
he didn't notice any switch in my English. And then I realized why. It's because
over the twenty years we've been together I've often used the same kind of
English with him, and sometimes he even uses it with me. It has become our
language of intimacy, a different sort of English that relates to family talk, the
30 language I grew up with.

So that you'll have some idea of what this family talk sounds like, I'll quote
what my mother said during a conversation that I videotaped and then
transcribed. During this conversation, she was talking about a political
gangster in Shanghai who had the same last name as her family's, Du, and how
in his early years the gangster wanted to be adopted by her family, who were
rich by comparison. Later, the gangster became more powerful, far richer than
my mother's family, and he showed up at my mother's wedding to pay his
respects. Here's what she said in part:

"Du Yusong having business like fruit stand. Like off-the-street kind. He is
40 Du like Du Zong—but not Tsung-ming Island people. The local people call
putong. The river east side, he belong to that side local people. That man want
to ask Du Zong father take him in like become own family. Du Zong father
wasn't look down on him, but didn't take seriously, until that man big like
become a mafia. Now important person, very hard to inviting him. Chinese
way, came only to show respect, don't stay for dinner. Respect for making big
celebration, he shows up. Mean gives lot of respect. Chinese custom. Chinese

---
[1] **nominalized:** in grammar or linguistics, converted into a noun.

2. ◀ REREAD Reread lines 9–21. Explain what Tan realized during her talk.
Support your answer with explicit textual evidence.

_____

_____

3. READ ▶ Read lines 31–49. In the margin, describe in your own words the
English spoken by Tan's mother.

© Houghton Mifflin Harcourt Publishing Company

> *But to me, my mother's English is perfectly clear, perfectly natural. It's my mother tongue.*

social life that way. If too important won't have to stay too long. He come to my wedding. I didn't see, I heard it. I gone to boy's side, they have YMCA dinner. Chinese age I was nineteen."

50   You should know that my mother's expressive command of English **belies**   **belies:**
how much she actually understands. She reads the *Forbes* report, listens to *Wall Street Week*, converses daily with her stockbroker, reads Shirley MacLaine's books with ease—all kinds of things I can't begin to understand. Yet some of my friends tell me they understand fifty percent of what my mother says. Some say they understand eighty to ninety percent. Some say they understand none of it, as if she were speaking pure Chinese.

But to me, my mother's English is perfectly clear, perfectly natural. It's my mother tongue. Her language, as I hear it, is vivid, direct, full of observation and imagery. That was the language that helped shape the way I saw things,
60   expressed things, made sense of the world.

Lately I've been giving more thought to the kind of English my mother speaks. Like others, I have described it to people as "broken" or "fractured" English. But I wince when I say that. It has always bothered me that I can

---

4.   ◀ **REREAD AND DISCUSS**   Reread lines 9–49. With a small group, discuss Tan's use of personal anecdotes. What does including her mother's story add to the essay?

5.   **READ** ▶   As you read lines 50–68, continue to cite textual evidence.

- Underline text that Tan uses to describe her mother's English.
- Circle text that shows how others perceive Tan's mother's English.

6.   ◀ **REREAD**   Reread lines 61–68. In the margin, explain Tan's position on "broken" English. Support your answer with explicit textual evidence.

© Houghton Mifflin Harcourt Publishing Company

think of no way to describe it other than "broken," as if it were damaged and needed to be fixed, as if it lacked a certain wholeness and soundness. I've heard other terms used, "limited English," for example. But they seem just as bad, as if everything is limited, including people's perceptions of the limited-English speaker.

70   I know this for a fact, because when I was growing up, my mother's "limited" English limited my perception of her. I was ashamed of her English. I believed that her English reflected the quality of what she had to say. That is, because she expressed them imperfectly, her thoughts were imperfect. And I had plenty of **empirical** evidence to support me: the fact that people in department stores, at banks, and in restaurants did not take her seriously, did not give her good service, pretended not to understand her, or even acted as if they did not hear her.

My mother has long realized the limitations of her English as well. When I was a teenager, she used to have me call people on the phone and pretend I was she. In this **guise,** I was forced to ask for information or even to complain and

80   yell at people who had been rude to her. One time it was a call to her stockbroker in New York. She had cashed out her small portfolio, and it just so happened we were going to New York the next week, our first trip outside California. I had to get on the phone and say in an adolescent voice that was not very convincing, "This is Mrs. Tan."

My mother was standing in the back whispering loudly, "Why he don't send me check, already two weeks late. So mad he lie to me, losing me money."

And then I said in perfect English on the phone, "Yes, I'm getting rather concerned. You had agreed to send the check two weeks ago, but it hasn't arrived."

90   Then she began to talk more loudly. "What he want, I come to New York tell him front of his boss, you cheating me?" And I was trying to calm her down, make her be quiet, while telling the stockbroker, "I can't tolerate any more excuses. If I don't receive the check immediately, I am going to have to speak to your manager when I'm in New York next week." And sure enough, the following week, there we were in front of this astonished stockbroker, and I was sitting there red-faced and quiet, and my mother, the real Mrs. Tan, was shouting at his boss in her impeccable broken English.

empirical:

guise:

7.   **READD ▶**   Read lines 69–97. Underline the evidence Tan uses to support her ideas about the limitations of her mother's English.

8.   **◀ REREAD**   Reread lines 77–97. In the margin, explain Tan's purpose for telling this story about her mother and the stockbroker.

© Houghton Mifflin Harcourt Publishing Company

We used a similar routine more recently, for a situation that was far less humorous. My mother had gone to the hospital for an appointment to find out about a CAT scan she had had a month earlier. She said she had spoken very good English, her best English, no mistakes. Still, she said, the hospital staff did not apologize when they informed her they had lost the CAT scan and she had come for nothing. She said they did not seem to have any sympathy when she told them she was anxious to know the exact diagnosis, since both her husband and her son had died of brain tumors. She said they would not give her any more information until the next time and she would have to make another appointment for that. So she said she would not leave until the doctor called her daughter. She wouldn't budge. And when the doctor finally called her daughter, me, who spoke in perfect English—lo and behold—we had assurances the CAT scan would be found, promises that a conference call on Monday would be held, and apologies for any suffering my mother had gone through for a most regrettable mistake.

I think my mother's English almost had an effect on limiting my possibilities in life as well. Sociologists and linguists probably will tell you that a person's developing language skills are more influenced by peers than by family. But I do think that the language spoken in the family, especially in immigrant families which are more insular, plays a large role in shaping the language of the child. And I believe that it affected my results on achievement tests, IQ tests, and the SAT. While my English skills were never judged poor, compared with math, English could not be considered my strong suit. In grade school I did moderately well, getting perhaps B's, sometimes B-pluses, in English and scoring perhaps in the sixtieth or seventieth percentile on achievement tests. But those scores were not good enough to override the opinion that my true abilities lay in math and science, because in those areas I achieved A's and scored in the ninetieth percentile or higher.

This was understandable. Math is precise; there is only one correct answer. Whereas, for me at least, the answers on English tests were always a judgment call, a matter of opinion and personal experience. Those tests were constructed around items like fill-in-the-blank sentence completion, such as "Even though

9. **READ** ▶ As you read lines 98–152, continue to cite textual evidence.

- Underline text that explains how Tan's mother's English "almost had an effect on limiting [Tan's] possibilities in life."
- In the margin, briefly note the examples Tan uses to support her position.

> *I began to write stories using all the Englishes I grew up with.*

bland:

130　Tom was _____ Mary thought he was _____.” And the correct answer always seemed to be the most **bland** combinations, for example, “Even though Tom was shy, Mary thought he was charming,” with the grammatical structure “even though” limiting the correct answer to some sort of opposites, so you wouldn't get answers like “Even though Tom was foolish, Mary thought he was ridiculous.” Well, according to my mother, there were very few limitations as to what Tom could have been and what Mary might have thought of him. So I never did well on tests like that.

　　　The same was true with word analogies, pairs of words for which you were supposed to find some logical semantic[2] relationship, for instance, “Sunset is to

140　nightfall as _____ is to _____.” And here you would be presented with a list of four possible pairs, one of which showed the same kind of relationship: *red* is to *stoplight, bus* is to *arrival, chills* is to *fever, yawn* is to *boring.* Well, I could never think that way. I knew what the tests were asking, but I could not block out of my mind the images already created by the first pair, *sunset* is to *nightfall*—and I would see a burst of colors against a darkening sky, the moon rising, the lowering of a curtain of stars. And all the other pairs of words—*red, bus, stoplight, boring*—just threw up a mass of confusing images, making it impossible for me to see that saying “A sunset precedes nightfall” was as logical as saying “A chill precedes a fever.” The only way I would have gotten that

150　answer right was to imagine an associative situation, such as my being

_____

[2] **semantic:** of or relating to language

© Houghton Mifflin Harcourt Publishing Company

disobedient and staying out past sunset, catching a chill at night, which turned into feverish pneumonia as punishment—which indeed did happen to me.

I have been thinking about all this lately, about my mother's English, about achievement tests. Because lately I've been asked, as a writer, why there are not more Asian-Americans represented in American literature. Why are there few Asian-Americans enrolled in creative writing programs? Why do so many Chinese students go into engineering? Well, these are broad sociological questions I can't begin to answer. But I have noticed in surveys—in fact, just last week—that Asian-American students, as a whole, do significantly better on 160 math achievement tests than on English tests. And this makes me think that there are other Asian-American students whose English spoken in the home might also be described as "broken" or "limited." And perhaps they also have teachers who are steering them away from writing and into math and science, which is what happened to me.

Fortunately, I happen to be rebellious and enjoy the challenge of disproving assumptions made about me. I became an English major my first year in college, after being enrolled as pre-med. I started writing nonfiction as a freelancer the week after I was told by my boss at the time that writing was my worst skill and I should hone my talents toward account management.

170 But it wasn't until 1985 that I began to write fiction. At first I wrote what I thought to be wittily crafted sentences, sentences that would finally prove I had mastery over the English language. Here's an example from the first draft of a story that later made its way into *The Joy Luck Club*, but without this line: "That was my mental quandary in its nascent state." A terrible line, which I can barely pronounce.

Fortunately, for reasons I won't get into here, I later decided I should envision a reader for the stories I would write. And the reader I decided on was my mother, because these were stories about mothers. So with this reader in mind—and in fact she did read my early drafts—I began to write stories using 180 all the Englishes I grew up with: the English I spoke to my mother, which for lack of a better term might he described as "simple"; the English she used with me, which for lack of a better term might be described as "broken"; my translation of her Chinese, which could certainly be described as "watered

10. **READ ▷** Read lines 153–169. Underline how other people reacted to Tan's English.

11. **◁ REREAD** Reread lines 153–164. In the margin, summarize Tan's main purpose in this paragraph. Support your answer with explicit textual evidence.

© Houghton Mifflin Harcourt Publishing Company

down"; and what I imagined to be her translation of her Chinese if she could speak in perfect English, her internal language, and for that I sought to preserve the essence, but neither an English nor a Chinese structure. I wanted to capture what language ability tests could never reveal: her intent, her passion, her imagery, the rhythms of her speech and the nature of her thoughts.

190 Apart from what any critic had to say about my writing, I knew I had succeeded where it counted when my mother finished reading my book and gave me her verdict: "So easy to read."

12. **READ ▶** Read lines 170–191. Underline the four types of English Tan describes. In the margin, explain why Tan finally felt she had succeeded.

SHORT RESPONSE

Cite Text Evidence Trace the structure of Tan's essay, describing both its organization and its methods. How does the structure of her essay support her purpose? **Cite evidence** from the text to support your response.

_____

_____

_____

_____

_____

_____

_____

_____

_____

_____

Background **Sherman Alexie** *is a poet, writer, and filmmaker who was raised on the Spokane Indian Reservation in Wellpinit, Washington. His work—which includes the acclaimed short story collection* The Lone Ranger and Tonto Fistfight in Heaven—*is largely inspired by his American Indian heritage and experiences. One of Alexie's recurring themes is the powerlessness many American Indians feel in contemporary society.*

Indian Boy Love Song (#2)

Poem by Sherman Alexie

CLOSE READ
Notes

1. **READD ▶** As you read lines 1–13, begin to collect and cite evidence.

   - Underline text describing what the speaker never did.
   - Circle adjectives describing people.

> I never spoke
> the language
> of the old women
>
> visiting my mother
> 5 in winters so cold
> they could freeze
> the tongue whole.
>
> I never held my head
> to their thin chests
> 10 believing in the heart.
>
> Indian women, forgive me.
> I grew up distant
> and always afraid.

© Houghton Mifflin Harcourt Publishing Company • Image Credits: ©Chris Felver/Getty Images; ©Katrina Brown/Alamy

2. ◀ **REREAD** Reread the poem. How would you describe the tone of the poem? Cite textual evidence in your response.

_____

_____

_____

_____

_____

_____

SHORT RESPONSE

Cite Text Evidence   What do you think is the theme of "Indian Boy Love Song (#2)"? What is the central idea about life or human nature that Alexie wants to communicate to his readers? **Cite textual evidence** in your response.

_____

_____

_____

_____

_____

_____

_____

_____

_____

_____

Building a Democracy

© Houghton Mifflin Harcourt Publishing Company • Image Credits: ©Volanthevist/Flickr/Getty Images

Building a Democracy

"A nation is formed by the willingness of each of us to share the responsibility for upholding the common good."

—Barbara Jordan

PUBLIC DOCUMENT
from The United States Constitution

PUBLIC DOCUMENT
Petition to the Massachusetts General Assembly
Prince Hall

HISTORY WRITING
Abigail Adams' Last Act of Defiance
Woody Holton

Background *The Constitution of the United States was written in September 1787 by a group of 55 men now known as the Framers of the Constitution, including George Washington and Benjamin Franklin. The document was written to replace the old Articles of Confederation and to establish the three branches of the federal government. The Constitution went into effect in 1789 and is considered the supreme law of the United States.*

from
The United States Constitution

Public Document

1. **READB▷** As you read lines 1–16, begin to collect and cite text evidence.

   - Circle the length of a presidential term.
   - Underline those who may *not* be appointed an Elector.
   - Make notes in the margin about who can hold the office of President.

CLOSE READ
Notes

ARTICLE. II.

Section. 1.

The executive Power shall be vested in a President of the United States of America. He shall hold his Office during the Term of four Years, and, together with the Vice President, chosen for the same Term, be elected, as follows:

Each State shall appoint, in such Manner as the Legislature thereof may direct, a Number of Electors, equal to the whole Number of Senators and Representatives to which the State may be entitled in the Congress: but no Senator or Representative, or Person holding an Office of Trust or Profit under the United States, shall be appointed an Elector.

The Congress may determine the Time of chusing the Electors, and the
10 Day on which they shall give their Votes; which Day shall be the same throughout the United States.

No Person except a natural born Citizen, or a Citizen of the United States, at the time of the Adoption of this Constitution, shall be eligible to the Office of President; neither shall any Person be eligible to that Office who shall not have attained to the Age of thirty five Years, and been fourteen Years a Resident within the United States.

The President shall, at stated Times, receive for his Services, a Compensation, which shall neither be increased nor diminished during the Period for which he shall have been elected, and he shall not receive within that

emolument: 20 Period any other **Emolument** from the United States, or any of them.

Before he enter on the Execution of his Office, he shall take the following Oath or Affirmation:—"I do solemnly swear (or affirm) that I will faithfully execute the Office of President of the United States, and will to the best of my Ability, preserve, protect and defend the Constitution of the United States."

Section. 2.

The President shall be Commander in Chief of the Army and Navy of the United States, and of the Militia of the several States, when called into the actual Service of the United States; he may require the Opinion, in writing, of the principal Officer in each of the executive Departments, upon any Subject relating to the Duties of their respective Offices, and he shall have Power to

30 grant Reprieves and Pardons for Offences against the United States, except in

impeachment: Cases of **Impeachment**.

He shall have Power, by and with the Advice and Consent of the Senate, to make Treaties, provided two thirds of the Senators present concur; and he shall nominate, and by and with the Advice and Consent of the Senate, shall appoint Ambassadors, other public Ministers and Consuls, Judges of the supreme

2. **◀ REREAD** Reread lines 12–16. Why do you think the Constitution places these particular limits on who may become President?

_____

_____

_____

_____

3. **READ ▶** As you read lines 17–54, continue to cite text evidence.

• Underline text that describes the President's executive power.

• Circle reasons for impeachment.

The United States Capitol, which houses Congress, is located on Capitol Hill, at the eastern end of the National Mall in Washington, DC.

Court, and all other Officers of the United States, whose Appointments are not herein otherwise provided for, and which shall be established by Law: but the Congress may by Law vest the Appointment of such inferior Officers, as they think proper, in the President alone, in the Courts of Law, or in the Heads

40 of Departments.

     The President shall have Power to fill up all Vacancies that may happen during the Recess of the Senate, by granting Commissions which shall expire at the End of their next Session.

Section. 3.

     He shall from time to time give to the Congress Information of the State of the Union, and recommend to their Consideration such Measures as he shall judge necessary and expedient; he may, on extraordinary Occasions, convene both Houses, or either of them, and in Case of Disagreement between them, with Respect to the Time of Adjournment, he may adjourn them to such Time as he shall think proper; he shall receive Ambassadors and other public

50 Ministers; he shall take Care that the Laws be faithfully executed, and shall Commission all the Officers of the United States.

© Houghton Mifflin Harcourt Publishing Company • Image Credits: ©SFC/Shutterstock

Section. 4.

The President, Vice President and all civil Officers of the United States, shall be removed from Office on Impeachment for, and Conviction of, Treason, Bribery, or other high Crimes and Misdemeanors.

4. ◀ REREAD AND DISCUSS In a small group, discuss the Presidential powers that you underlined in lines 17–54. For every executive power that the President has, discuss the Senate's role in the decision-making process.

SHORT RESPONSE

Cite Text Evidence   Analyze how the authors structured this part of the Constitution. How does this part of the Constitution uphold the principles of a respreentative democracy, a separation of powers, and a system of checks and balances? Review your reading notes. Be sure to **cite text evidence** in your response.

_____

_____

_____

_____

_____

_____

_____

_____

_____

_____

© Houghton Mifflin Harcourt Publishing Company

Background Prince Hall *(1735–1807) was held as a slave by William Hall, in Boston until the age of 35, when he was freed. Hall used his freedom to become an advocate for African Americans. Hall made many petitions on behalf of free blacks and successfully petitioned for the release of three Boston African Americans who had been kidnapped into slavery. For years, Hall protested that African American children did not have public schools, and eventually he started a school of his own for them.*

Petition to the Massachusetts General Assembly

Public Document by Prince Hall

1. **READD** As you read the petition, begin to collect and cite text evidence.

    - In the margin, paraphrase the first sentence (lines 3–10).
    - Underline three of Hall's premises that support his argument against slavery.
    - In the margin on the next page, analyze what Hall means by "the natural right of all men" (line 30).

CLOSE READ
Notes

To the Honorable Counsel and House of Representatives for the State of Massachusetts Bay in General Court assembled, January 13, 1777:

The petition of a great number of blacks detained in a state of slavery in a free and Christian county humbly points out that your petitioners understand that they have in common with all other men a natural and unalienable right to that freedom which the Great Parent of the Universe bestowed equally on all mankind, and which they have never forfeited by any compact or agreement whatever, but that they were unjustly dragged by the hand of cruel power along with their dearest friends, and some of them even torn from the embraces of

10   their tender parents, from a populous, pleasant, and plentiful country. In violation of Laws of Nature and of Nations and in defiance of all the tender feelings of humanity, they were brought here to be sold like beasts of burden, and like them condemned to slavery for life among a people professing the mild religion of Jesus—a people not insensible of the secrets of rational being nor without spirit to resent the unjust endeavors of others to reduce *them* to a state of bondage and **subjugation**. Your Honors need not to be informed that a life of slavery like that of your petitioners, deprived of every social

subjugation:

privilege and of every thing requisite to render life tolerable, is far worse than nonexistence.

20   In imitation of the laudable example of the good people of these states, your petitioners have long and patiently waited the outcome of petition after petition presented by them to the Legislative Body of this state, and with grief reflect that their lack of success has been similar each time. They cannot but express their astonishment that it has never been considered that every principle from which America has acted in the course of their unhappy difficulties with Great Britain pleads stronger than a thousand arguments in favor of your petitioners. They therefore humbly beseech Your Honors to give this petition its due weight and consideration and cause an act of the legislature to be passed whereby they may be restored to the enjoyments which is the

30   natural right of all men and that their children, who were born in this Land of Liberty, may not be held as slaves after they arrive at the age of twenty-one years. So may the inhabitants of this State no longer be guilty of the inconsistency of acting in ways that they condemn and oppose in others. May they prosper in their present glorious struggle for Liberty and have those blessings to them.

2. ◀ **REREAD AND DISCUSS** Reread the petition. Circle Hall's purpose for this petition. Explain the three main premises that support his reasoning.

_____

_____

SHORT RESPONSE

Cite Text Evidence Summarize the purpose and premises of Hall's argument. Review your reading notes, and be sure to **cite text evidence** in your response.

_____

_____

_____

_____

_____

_____

© Houghton Mifflin Harcourt Publishing Company

Background Abigail Smith Adams *(1744–1818) was the daughter of liberal Congregational minister, William Smith. She was considered too sickly for formal education, but was taught at home and had access to her father's library. She was embarrassed by her poor spelling and punctuation, yet was known for her intelligence and passion for the cause of women's rights. The Adams family was the first one to live in the White House. Abigail was nicknamed "Her Majesty" because of her perceived influence over her husband.*

Abigail Adams' Last
Act of Defiance

History Writing by Woody Holton

CLOSE READ
Notes

1. **READ** ▶ As you read lines 1–19, begin to cite and collect text evidence.

   - Underline references to dates and events that orient the reader and provide historical context.
   - Circle the main idea in lines 1–9 and in lines 10–19.
   - In the margin, summarize the situation that concerns Adams.

Weeks before the Continental Congress issued the Declaration of Independence in 1776, Abigail Adams penned a now famous letter to her husband, John, admonishing him to "Remember the Ladies" when drawing up a new code of laws. "If perticuliar care and attention is not paid to the Laidies," she wrote, "we are determined to **foment** a Rebelion, and will not hold ourselves bound by any Laws in which we have no voice, or Representation." Within a few years of writing these words, Adams did something that has never been revealed until now. She carried out a mini-revolution in the arena that mattered to her the most: her own household.

10   Of all the means by which the Founding Fathers and other men lorded it over women, none annoyed Adams more than the legal degradation that women had to submit to the moment they got married. Single women, including widows, were allowed to own and control property. Yet as Adams

foment:

> " ... scratching out the four-page document was the ultimate act of rebellion. "

complained to her husband in a June 1782 letter, wives' property was "subject to the controul and disposal of our partners, to whom the Laws have given a soverign Authority." Historians have studied Abigail Adams' denunciations of married women's inability to control property for decades. But what they have overlooked is that she did not simply complain about the government's denial of married women's property rights. She defied it.

20   As the Revolutionary War drew to a close, Adams started setting aside a portion of her husband's property and declaring it her own. She added more and more to this stash over the ensuing decades, and she invested it wisely. By the end of 1815 her "pocket money," as she sometimes called it, had grown to more than $5,000—which would be about $100,000 today.

Finally in 1816, racked with pain and convinced she was dying, Adams delivered the parting shot in her household revolution. On January 18, she sat down to write a will. Since she had no legal right as a married woman to own property in her name and her husband was still very much alive, scratching out the four-page document was the ultimate act of rebellion. Moreover, a close

2. (REREAD) Reread lines 10–19. In what way did the laws for single women and married women differ? Support your answer with explicit textual evidence.

_____

_____

_____

_____

3. (READ ▷) As you read lines 20–55, continue to cite text evidence.

• Circle actions of Adams that were caused by the government's denial of property rights for married women.

• Underline references to dates that show the order in which events occurred.

© Houghton Mifflin Harcourt Publishing Company

This portrait of Adams was painted by Benjamin Blythe in 1766, when she was 22 years old.

30 look at the will reveals a curious fact that historians have mostly ignored. Apart from a couple of token gifts to her two sons, all the people Adams chose to bequeath money to were women. And many of those women were married.

Adams' personal property rights revolution had its roots in her struggle to shield her family from the financial destruction that accompanied the Revolutionary War. Of all the patriot soldiers and statesmen who were forced to abandon their families for long periods, few stayed away as long as John Adams, who saw very little of his Braintree, Mass., farm from 1774 to 1784. John put Abigail in charge of all of the Adams family finances, and she ended up handling her husband's money much better than he ever had, primarily

40 because she was more open to risk. During the course of the war she became an

4. **◀ REREAD** Reread lines 25–32. Why does Holton call writing a will "the ultimate act of rebellion"? Support your answer with explicit textual evidence.

_____

_____

_____

© Houghton Mifflin Harcourt Publishing Company • Image Credits: ©Bettmann/Corbis

CLOSE READ
Notes

depreciate:

envoy:

import merchant and then a speculator in **depreciated** government securities and Vermont land titles. And as she repeatedly reinvested her profits, she increasingly thought of the money she earned as her own.

Abigail lived by the credo "nothing venture nothing have"—a notion that John found somewhat alarming. While he was an **envoy** in France, the couple confronted a seemingly mundane problem. How could he remit a portion of his salary home? Her solution was audacious. If he shipped her trunkloads of merchandise from Europe, she could extract the few items her family needed and arrange to sell the rest to New England shopkeepers whose shelves were

50 nearly empty because of the war. She convinced John the scheme would allow her to avoid having to "pay extravagant prices" for basic necessities, downplaying that she could also turn a healthy profit by selling the imported goods at an enormous markup. When some of these shipments were captured by the British, John wanted to abandon the whole thing, but she wrote back, "If one in 3 arrives I should be a gainer."

Nearly all of Abigail Adams' biographers mention her will, but they usually move on, overlooking not only the remarkable fact of its existence but its contents. In it, she made token gifts to her two surviving sons, but she gave nothing to her grandsons, nephews or male servants. Everything went to her

60 granddaughters, nieces, female servants and daughters-in-law. In addition to gowns and small sums of cash to pay for mourning rings, Abigail handed out more than $4,000 worth of bank stock, a $1,200 IOU and a total of seven shares of stock in the companies managing the Weymouth and Haverhill toll bridges.

5. **READ ▷** As you read lines 56–96, continue to cite text evidence.

- In the margin of lines 56–63 explain Adams's solution to the problem regarding women's property rights.

- Circle evidence that shows that Adams's family supported her "mini-revolution."

- In the lines below, analyze the structure of lines 70–85. How does the author organize the facts he presents in these lines?

_____

_____

_____

_____

32

© Houghton Mifflin Harcourt Publishing Company

> "Louisa acknowledged what the law of the land denied and Abigail had always affirmed: that the money was hers to give."

© Houghton Mifflin Harcourt Publishing Company

There is no indication that Adams had any **animus** against her male relatives. So why did she exclude all but two of them from her will? Having spent three decades asserting control over land and ownership of personal property despite being married, Adams now bequeathed the bulk of her estate to her granddaughters, nieces, daughters-in-law and female servants in order to enable them, as far as lay in her power, to make the same claim.

70   To her own surprise, Abigail held on for another year and a half after writing her will. She died about 1 p.m. on October 28, 1818, a few weeks shy of her 74th birthday. Abigail's will was not a legal document that any court was bound to respect, and John would have been within his rights in throwing it in the fire. But he honored it to the letter.

     Abigail had assigned her son Thomas the responsibility of supervising the distribution of her property. Thomas' brother, John Quincy Adams, and their father assisted him in carrying out Abigail's wishes. On November 9, less than two weeks after her death, John transferred the $1,200 promissory note to Louisa Smith [Abigail's neice and steadfast companion], just as Abigail had

80   directed. The former president's compliance with the provisions of his wife's will transformed it into a legally valid document. In the eyes of the law, she had acted as his agent and distributed property that belonged to him. In 1819 John Quincy replaced the promissory note he had given his mother years earlier with a new one made out to Louisa herself. No one could ever challenge his cousin's legal right to recover these funds, for she had never married.

animus:

bequest:

In January 1819, when Louisa Catherine Adams, John Quincy's wife, learned that Abigail had left her an inheritance of $150, she set aside half of the **bequest** to be divided equally among her three sons, who seemed "to have a better title to it than I could boast." By passing this money on to Abigail's
90 grandsons, Louisa may have indicated disapproval of her mother-in-law's decision to exclude all male descendants other than her own sons from her will. Yet it seems unlikely that Abigail would have considered the younger woman's gift a defeat. After all, by deciding on her own authority to present the money to her children instead of her husband, Louisa acknowledged what the law of the land denied and Abigail had always affirmed: that the money was hers to give.

6. **◀ REREAD** Reread lines 86–96. Explain the author's assertion that Adams would not consider it a defeat that Louisa Catherine Adams bequeathed part of her inheritance to her sons.

_____

_____

_____

_____

SHORT RESPONSE

Cite Text Evidence   What problem did Adams confront and what was her solution? Review your reading notes, and be sure to **cite text evidence** in your response.

_____

_____

_____

_____

_____

_____

_____

© Houghton Mifflin Harcourt Publishing Company

© Houghton Mifflin Harcourt Publishing Company o Image Credits: ©Max Oppenheim/Stone/Getty Images

The Individual and Society

The Individual and Society

"Trust thyself: every heart vibrates
to that iron string."

—Ralph Waldo Emerson

© Houghton Mifflin Harcourt Publishing Company ● Image Credits: ©Max Oppenheim/Stone/Getty Images

Background *Less than a hundred years after the United States was founded, the new nation discovered its voice in a poet who spoke to all the world. His name was* **Walt Whitman,** *and he struck a note in literature that was as forthright, as original, and as deeply charged with democracy's energies as the land that produced him.*

Poems by
Walt Whitman

I Hear America Singing . . . . Walt Whitman

A Noiseless Patient Spider . . . . Walt Whitman

Walt Whitman *(1819–1892) grew up in rural Long Island and crowded Brooklyn. He held a series of jobs including typesetter, printer, newspaper editor, school teacher, carpenter, and journalist. In the 1840s, Whitman published a number of poems and short stories—and even a fairly successful novel—but these were conventional efforts. Whitman was just waiting for the proper inspiration. Upon reading Ralph Waldo Emerson, he realized that he could celebrate all aspects of nature and humanity by using spiritual language. "I was simmering, simmering, simmering," he once declared. "Emerson brought me to a boil."*

In the early 1850s, Whitman quit his job as a journalist and worked on a book of poems called Leaves of Grass. *Many people were shocked by its controversial content and revolutionary form. Of the 800 copies printed, most were eventually thrown away. However, a few readers recognized the poet's genius. In a letter to Whitman, Emerson called* Leaves of Grass *"the most extraordinary piece of wit and wisdom that America has yet contributed."*

© Houghton Mifflin Harcourt Publishing Company • Image Credits: ©Hulton Archive/Getty Images; ©AP Photo; ©Bettmann/Corbis

1. **READ ▶** As you read lines 1–11, begin to collect and cite text evidence.

   • Underline the different kinds of workers the poem catalogs.
   • Circle the word that refers to the collective group of singers.
   • In the margin, note the type of people the speaker "hears."

I Hear America Singing

I hear America singing, the varied carols I hear,
Those of mechanics, each one singing his as it should be blithe
    and strong,
The carpenter singing his as he measures his plank or beam,
The mason singing his as he makes ready for work, or leaves off
    work,
5 The boatman singing what belongs to him in his boat, the
    deckhand singing on the steamboat deck,
The shoemaker singing as he sits on his bench, the hatter singing
    as he stands,
The wood-cutter's song, the ploughboy's on his way in the
    morning, or at noon intermission or at sundown,
The delicious singing of the mother, or of the young wife at work,
    or of the girl sewing or washing,
Each singing what belongs to him or her and to none else,
10 The day what belongs to the day—at night the party of young
    fellows, robust, friendly,
Singing with open mouths their strong melodious songs.

2. **◀ REREAD** Reread lines 10–11. What attitude does the speaker express toward the young men? Cite evidence from the text in your response.

_____

_____

_____

_____

_____

_____

© Houghton Mifflin Harcourt Publishing Company

SHORT RESPONSE

Cite Text Evidence   What is the theme of this poem—what is the author revealing about America? **Cite text evidence** in your response.

_____

_____

_____

_____

_____

_____

_____

_____

_____

© Houghton Mifflin Harcourt Publishing Company • Image Credits: ©Alison Shaw/Corbis

1. **READ ▶** As you read lines 1–10, begin to collect and cite text evidence.

   - Underline the two subjects the speaker observes.
   - Circle references to web-making.
   - In the margin, explain what surrounds the "noiseless patient spider." and "you O my soul."

A Noiseless Patient Spider

A noiseless patient spider,
I mark'd where on a little promontory[1] it stood isolated,
Mark'd how to explore the vacant vast surrounding,
It launch'd forth filament, filament, filament, out of itself,
5   Ever unreeling them, ever tirelessly speeding them.

And you O my soul where you stand,
Surrounded, detached, in measureless oceans of space,
Ceaselessly musing, venturing, throwing, seeking the spheres to
        connect them,
Till the bridge you will need be form'd, till the ductile[2] anchor
        hold,
10   Till the gossamer[3] thread you fling catch somewhere, O my soul.

---

[1] **promontory:** a ridge of land or rock jutting out over water or land.
[2] **ductile:** capable of being drawn or stretched out.
[3] **gossamer:** extremely light or fine.

2. **◀ REREAD AND DISCUSS** Reread lines 1–10. With a small group, discuss the use of parallelism in lines 5 and 8. What do these parallel elements suggest about the relationship between the spider and the speaker?

SHORT RESPONSE

Cite Text Evidence   What is the theme of the poem? What details communicate that theme? **Cite text evidence** in your response.

_____

_____

_____

_____

_____

© Houghton Mifflin Harcourt Publishing Company

Background *As the acknowledged leader of the transcendentalists,* **Ralph Waldo Emerson** *(1803–1882) was a towering figure in the 19th-century literary world. He helped shape a new, uniquely American body of literature and is often cited as one of the most significant writers in American history. "All life is an experiment," the radical thinker and writer once said. "The more experiments you make, the better."*

Essays by
Ralph Waldo Emerson

***from* Nature** . . . . Ralph Waldo Emerson

***from* Self-Reliance** . . . . Ralph Waldo Emerson

Ralph Waldo Emerson *was born in Boston, Massachusetts, in 1803. He attended Harvard and was ordained as a Unitarian minister in 1829. Just over a year later, his beloved wife, Ellen, died of tuberculosis. Ellen's death threw Emerson into a state of spiritual crisis. In 1832, after much consideration, Emerson resigned his post. He settled in Concord, Massachusetts, and devoted himself to the study of philosophy, religion, and literature.*

In 1836 Emerson published Nature, *in which he eloquently articulated his transcendental philosophy, an outgrowth of European romanticism. That same year, Emerson formed the Transcendental Club with a group of like-minded friends, including Henry David Thoreau and Margaret Fuller.* Nature, *with its emphasis on self-reliance and individuality, became the group's unofficial manifesto. He elaborated upon his ideas in essays and a series of popular lectures. By the 1840s, the Sage of Concord, as he was known, had become a major literary force whose influence is still evident in American culture today.*

© Houghton Mifflin Harcourt Publishing Company • Image Credits: ©Anetlanphoto/Shutterstock, ©Bettmann/Corbis

1. **READ ▶** As you read lines 1–20, begin to collect and cite evidence.

   - Underline metaphorical phrases.
   - Circle language that Emerson uses to describe the woods.
   - In the margin, explain what event causes the author "perfect exhilaration" (lines 2–5).

from Nature

Nature is a setting that fits equally well a comic or a mourning piece. In good health, the air is a cordial of incredible virtue. Crossing a bare common, in snow puddles, at twilight, under a clouded sky, without having in my thoughts any occurrence of special good fortune, I have enjoyed a perfect exhilaration. I am glad to the brink of fear. In the woods too, a man casts off his years, as the snake his slough,[1] and at what period soever of life, is always a child. In the woods, is perpetual youth. Within these plantations of God, a **decorum** and sanctity reign, a perennial festival is dressed, and the guest sees not how he should tire of them in a thousand years. In the woods, we return to reason and faith. There I feel that nothing can befall me in life,—no disgrace, no calamity, (leaving me my eyes,) which nature cannot repair. Standing on the bare ground,—my head bathed by the blithe air, and uplifted into infinite space,—all mean egotism vanishes. I become a transparent eye-ball; I am nothing; I see all; the currents of the Universal Being circulate through me; I am part or particle of God. The name of the nearest friend sounds then foreign and accidental: to be brothers, to be acquaintances,—master or servant, is then a trifle and a disturbance. I am the lover of uncontained and immortal

decorum:

10

---
[1] **slough:** the cast-off skin of a snake.

2. **◀ REREAD** Reread lines 5–15. How is a man "always a child" in the woods? Which sentence acts as a central idea and best supports this metaphor?

_____

_____

_____

_____

3. **READ ▶** As you read lines 21–35, continue to cite textual evidence.

   - Underline the topic sentence Emerson uses to introduce each paragraph.
   - In the margin, explain what the "colors of the spirit" refers to (line 32).
   - Circle examples of personification.

© Houghton Mifflin Harcourt Publishing Company

beauty. In the wilderness, I find something more dear and connate[2] than in streets or villages. In the tranquil landscape, and especially in the distant line
20 of the horizon, man beholds somewhat as beautiful as his own nature.

The greatest delight which the fields and woods minister, is the suggestion of an **occult** relation between man and the vegetable. I am not alone and unacknowledged. They nod to me, and I to them. The waving of the boughs in the storm, is new to me and old. It takes me by surprise, and yet is not unknown. Its effect is like that of a higher thought or a better emotion coming over me, when I deemed I was thinking justly or doing right.

Yet it is certain that the power to produce this delight, does not reside in nature, but in man, or in a harmony of both. It is necessary to use these pleasures with great temperance. For, nature is not always tricked[3] in holiday
30 attire, but the same scene which yesterday breathed perfume and glittered as for the frolic of the nymphs, is overspread with melancholy today. Nature always wears the colors of the spirit. To a man laboring under calamity, the heat of his own fire hath sadness in it. Then, there is a kind of contempt of the landscape felt by him who has just lost by death a dear friend. The sky is less grand as it shuts down over less worth in the population.

occult:

---

[2] **connate:** agreeable; able to be related to.
[3] **tricked:** dressed.

---

4. ◀ **REREAD AND DISCUSS** Reread lines 21–35. With a small group, discuss what Emerson is referring to when he alludes to the relationship between "man and the vegetable."

SHORT RESPONSE

Cite Text Evidence Write an objective summary of the piece by restating the central ideas in your own words. Be sure that your objective summary is free from personal opinions and **cite text evidence** in your response.

_____

_____

_____

_____

_____

_____

© Houghton Mifflin Harcourt Publishing Company

1. **READ ▶** As you read lines 1–24, begin to collect and cite evidence.

   - Underline the topic sentence in each paragraph.
   - In the margin, explain the central idea of lines 1–11.
   - Circle the response of the "valued adviser."

from Self-Reliance

There is a time in every man's education when he arrives at the conviction that envy is ignorance; that imitation is suicide; that he must take himself for better for worse as his portion; that though the wide universe is full of good, no kernel of nourishing corn can come to him but through his toil bestowed on that plot of ground which is given to him to till. . . .

Trust thyself: every heart vibrates to that iron string. Accept the place the divine providence has found for you, the society of your contemporaries, the connection of events. Great men have always done so, and confided themselves childlike to the genius of their age, betraying their perception that the
10 absolutely trustworthy was seated at their heart, working through their hands, predominating in all their being . . . .

nonconformist:

Whoso would be a man, must be a **nonconformist**. He who would gather immortal palms[1] must not be hindered by the name of goodness, but must explore if it be goodness. Nothing is at last sacred but the integrity of your own mind. Absolve you to yourself, and you shall have the suffrage[2] of the world. I remember an answer which when quite young I was prompted to make to a valued adviser who was wont to importune[3] me with the dear old doctrines of the church. On my saying, "What have I to do with the sacredness of traditions, if I live wholly from within?" my friend suggested—"But these impulses may be
20 from below, not from above." I replied, "They do not seem to me to be such; but

---

[1] **immortal palms:** everlasting triumph and honor. In ancient times, people carried palm leaves as a symbol of victory, success, or joy.
[2] **suffrage:** approval, support.
[3] **importune:** ask persistently.

---

2. **◀ REREAD** Reread lines 12–24 and restate the central idea.

_____

_____

_____

_____

© Houghton Mifflin Harcourt Publishing Company

if I am the Devil's child, I will live then from the Devil." No law can be sacred to me but that of my nature. Good and bad are but names very readily transferable to that or this; the only right is what is after my **constitution**; the only wrong what is against it . . . .

What I must do is all that concerns me, not what the people think. This rule, equally arduous in actual and in intellectual life, may serve for the whole distinction between greatness and **meanness**. It is the harder because you will always find those who think they know what is your duty better than you know it. It is easy in the world to live after the world's opinion; it is easy in solitude to
30 live after our own; but the great man is he who in the midst of the crowd keeps with perfect sweetness the independence of solitude . . . .

For nonconformity the world whips you with its displeasure. And therefore a man must know how to estimate a sour face. The by-standers look askance on him in the public street or in the friend's parlor. If this aversion had its origin in contempt and resistance like his own he might well go home with a sad countenance; but the sour faces of the multitude, like their sweet faces, have no deep cause, but are put on and off as the wind blows and a newspaper directs . . . .

The other terror that scares us from self-trust is our consistency; a
40 reverence for our past act or word because the eyes of others have no other data for computing our orbit than our past acts, and we are loth to disappoint them . . . .

A foolish consistency is the hobgoblin of little minds, adored by little statesmen and philosophers and divines. With consistency a great soul has simply nothing to do. He may as well concern himself with his shadow on the wall. Speak what you think now in hard words and tomorrow speak what

constitution:

meanness:

3. **READ ▷** As you read lines 25–38, continue to collect and cite evidence.

 • Underline the topic sentence in each paragraph.

 • In the margin, explain common reactions to noncomformists.

4. **READ ▷** Read lines 39–51. Underline text that explains why we are reluctant to trust ourselves.

© Houghton Mifflin Harcourt Publishing Company

tomorrow thinks in hard words again, though it contradict everything you said today.—"Ah, so you shall be sure to be misunderstood."—Is it so bad then to be misunderstood? Pythagoras was misunderstood, and Socrates, and Jesus, and

50 Luther, and Copernicus, and Galileo, and Newton,[4] and every pure and wise spirit that ever took flesh. To be great is to be misunderstood.

[4] **Pythagoras was misunderstood, and Socrates, and Jesus, and Luther, and Copernicus, and Galileo, and Newton:** great thinkers whose radical theories and viewpoints caused controversy.

5. **◄ REREAD** Reread lines 39–51. Which sentence best summarizes the central idea of this part of the essay?

_____

_____

_____

_____

_____

_____

SHORT RESPONSE

Cite Text Evidence Write an objective summary of the piece by restating the central ideas in your own words. Be sure that your objective summary is free from personal opinions. **Cite text evidence**.

_____

_____

_____

_____

_____

_____

_____

© Houghton Mifflin Harcourt Publishing Company

Background *The following article was written by* **David Gessner**, *a contributing editor to* OnEarth *magazine. In it, he explains his change of opinion about Cape Wind, the first federally approved offshore wind farm. The note accompanying the article, published in December 2011, reads: "It's been 10 years since a proposal was submitted to build America's first offshore wind farm in Nantucket Sound off Cape Cod. The federal government finally approved the project earlier this year, although court battles continue to delay construction. After a decade of division, our contributing editor [Gessner] shares his personal journey of acceptance."*

Spoiling Walden

Or, How I Learned to Stop Worrying and Love Cape Wind

Essay by David Gessner

CLOSE READ
Notes

1. **READD ▶** As you read lines 1–17, begin to collect and cite text evidence.

   • Circle the two things the author loves in lines 1–9.
   • Underline loaded language the author uses to describe his first reaction to the wind farm proposal.
   • In the margin, explain Gessner's initial opposition to the wind farm.

Let's start with love. A good place to start, yes? In this case love of a place and love of a book. The book is *Walden*[1] by Henry David Thoreau, which I read as a young man, and the place is Cape Cod, or, more specifically, the East Dennis beaches I have been coming to since I was very young. My love of those beaches is, at first, a young man's love, but later it grows into something deeper. Inspired in part by Thoreau's book, I move there after college and work part-time as a carpenter while writing my own first book. Though I have now lived all over the country, it is still the first place I think of when people mention "home." It is my Walden and Cape Cod Bay is my Walden Pond.

10   So of course when someone—a businessman no less—suggests that he wants to place 130 wind turbines—bird-killing turbines!—in Nantucket Sound off the shores of my Walden, I react with outrage. Not in my backyard? Not in my backyard! This is a sacred place, a place apart, and if this is a sacred place then these wind turbines are, as I tell anyone who will listen, a desecration.

---

[1] *Walden*: Thoreau's book about his time living simply and self-sufficiently in nature.

I cling to this position for years, holding tight, but then, gradually, my grip starts to loosen. Some things happen, some things change. The story of those things, those happenings and changes, is the story of my wind journey.

One thing I do is to move away from Cape Cod, and so I start seeing the place I still consider home from a distance, from arm's length, while at the same time seeing how that place connects to others. Another thing I do is start to travel extensively, reporting for an environmental magazine. I visit Cape Breton in Nova Scotia, which seems like driving onto Cape Cod a hundred years ago, until I reach a city called Sydney Mines. The city looks like it has been cracked open and had its insides sucked out, which it turns out, is pretty much what happened. In Mike's Place Pub & Grill, I talk to a local man named Keith who tells me the story of the town's glory years, when it supplied coal for much of Canada, and of the depths to which the town fell after the coal was gone.

2. **◀ REREAD** Reread lines 15–17. What do these lines explain about Gessner's approach to the topic? Support your answer with explicit textual evidence.

_____

_____

_____

_____

3. **READ ▶** As you read lines 18–35, underline the first two things Gessner does on his "wind journey."

4. **◀ REREAD** Reread lines 21–35. What can you infer about the comment that the only jobs left in Sydney Mines were funeral directors? Why does Gessner include this conversation with Keith?

_____

_____

_____

_____

_____

"The coal was gone and they had taken everything out of the town. Where
it had been wall-to-wall with people on a Saturday night you suddenly couldn't
find anyone. Maybe a stray dog and a single taxi. A ghost town."

His eyes drooped as if in sympathy with the town. His voice sounded
beautiful, his accent vaguely Irish.

"There were no jobs, you see. Other than funeral directors. There was a big
call for those."

The more I travelled, the more I found men like Keith and places like
Sydney Mines. Places hollowed out and then deserted. I began to think more,
not just about beautiful places, but about what we extract from them. This
culminated last summer when I travelled along the Gulf Coast during the
height, or depths, of the BP oil spill. There I found the most intense
juxtaposition of beauty and energy as I spent mornings birdwatching—seeing
roseate spoonbills and ibises—near Halliburton Road and oil refineries, or
spent a night out in a fish camp, a few hundred yards from a fringe of marsh
that appeared burned, but was, in fact, oiled.

juxtaposition:

---

5. **READ ▶** As you read lines 36–69, continue to cite textual evidence.

• Underline text that shows how Gessner connects Cape Cod and the Gulf
Coast.
• In the margin of lines 45–62, explain how Gessner connects modern people
to Thoreau and his personal math.

The place was stunningly beautiful, and for the Cajun fishermen I met, like Ryan Lambert, it was their Walden. But it was also slathered in the substance that we all use to power our lives. The Gulf has been called "a national sacrifice zone," and it seemed to have been sacrificed so that the rest of us could keep on living the way we live. I thought to myself: this place is connected to Cape Cod. Not metaphorically, but literally, by its waters.

And I thought, because I could not help but think of it, of energy. Where we get our energy from and how we pay for it, in the broadest sense. As a birdwatcher, I know that every animal is required to do the math of energy in its own way, and humans, whatever we may think, are not exempt. It was Thoreau, our patron saint of frugality, who created the initial ledger sheet, the personal math that many of us have begun to think about again during these difficult times, the calculus of our own input and output. In *Walden* he did his figuring right there on the page for us. *Here is how much I spent and here is what I gained.* It is the same math that animals rely on instinctively when they hunt. By Thoreau's reasoning, human lives, like the lives of other animals, require a strict mathematical relationship with energy, its gains and losses, its conservation and squandering.

Years ago, on Cape Cod, I had been quick to embrace, and mimic, Thoreau's love of nature but slow to hear his sterner message of personal responsibility. I rationalized this by saying that I preferred Thoreau the celebrator to Thoreau the preacher. But in the Gulf I found myself returning to the other, stricter Thoreau. His relationship with energy was simple but

---

6. **◄ REREAD** Reread lines 51–69. Circle the three titles Gessner gives to Thoreau. Why does Gessner come to prefer the stricter Thoreau?

_____

_____

_____

_____

_____

_____

> *The place was stunningly beautiful . . . it was their Walden.*

profound: instead of just focusing on getting more, he limited his input and refined his output.

As I travelled through the Gulf, I also thought back to a meeting I'd had two summers before. A friend had put me in touch with Jim Gordon, the president of Cape Wind, and we met for lunch in Hyannis before driving out to one of the beaches that would face out toward the hundred-plus turbine towers that would make up the wind farm. The beach was crammed with people, umbrellas sprouting and kids running this way and that, and once we got to the shore we looked out past kids on inflatable rafts and roaring Jet Skis and powerboats to where the towers would stand on the horizon. One of the arguments that wind opponents have made is that putting wind turbines out in this water would be like putting them in the Grand Canyon. Jim, consciously or not, was using this beach as both prop and stage, and the message was clear: *this ain't the Grand Canyon.*

The question many have asked is: does having a wind farm out on the horizon detract from that elemental experience of the beach? The argument that Jim Gordon was making, without saying a word, was that this experience was already limited enough, and that the site of blades blowing in the breeze was not going to detract from it one iota.

Now Jim held up his thumb against the horizon.

---

7. **READER ▶** As you read lines 70–111, continue to cite textual evidence.

   • Underline what Gessner sees on the beach.
   • In the margin of lines 70–86, explain why the beach is already "limited enough."
   • Circle Jim Gordon's statements about why the turbines should be seen.

"From here the turbines will be six or seven miles out. They'll be about as big as my thumbnail."

90   This, of course, was another big point of contention. How big would they really look from the shore? And what would it mean for Cape Codders to look out at their theoretically wild waters and see what would be, for all its techno grace, an industrial site? While I had deep sympathy with the **aesthetic** point of view, it was hard to argue that windmills that would appear a few inches tall on the horizon would ruin the place's wildness.

aesthetic:

    And with what Jim said next, he almost won me over entirely. "We need to connect the dots," he said.

    Connect the dots. Wasn't that what Thoreau had tried to do? Wasn't that the definition of ecology?

100   "We would barely see the turbines from here, but maybe we should see them," he continued. "It's what we can't see that's killing us. Like the particle emissions from the power plant in Sandwich. And the oil being shipped to run that plant."

    He shook his head and stared out at the horizon where his windmills would turn. "Maybe it's not such a bad idea for us to see just where our energy is coming from," he said.

    I nodded. At the time my thoughts on wind power were still in flux. But with this I could not disagree. I still was, and still am, worried that migrating birds might run into the turbines. A million birds a night migrate over the

110 Cape during the fall migration, and I fret that by supporting wind I am becoming an avian Judas. But it is a time of tough choices.

---

8. **◀ REREAD** Reread lines 96–99. How does the point Jim Gordon makes in these lines influence Gessner?

_____

_____

_____

_____

_____

> *...if there are Waldens then they are all interconnected.*

"Do you know the windfarms will kill more birds in a year than were killed during the whole Gulf disaster?" a wind opponent said to me recently. This "statistic," of course, hinges on a very narrow definition of bird fatalities. My accuser was not thinking of habitat destruction and warming, and the whole host of other consequences of the rabid pursuit of oil. Meanwhile, Jim Gordon's camp claims that the slow-moving and well-lit turbines should prove less of a threat to birds than most tall buildings.

120 I am not sure of that. What I am sure of is that there are no more Waldens, or, more accurately, if there are Waldens then they are all interconnected. Cape Cod has been called "a place apart." I am writing this from Cape Cod right now, and I understand what the phrase means: the land of this fragile ex-peninsula is very specific to itself, and when you come here, and cross the bridge, you leave other places behind and enter a place like nowhere else.

But I can no longer use this term to describe the Cape. It is not apart from the fragile Louisiana fish camp where I spent the night, oil lapping nearby, and it is not apart from Sydney Mines. Each place in this threatened world, separate but connected, must now make an accounting, keep its own ledger sheet with a cold and honest eye. We hold onto our pristine place by sacrificing other places. 130 I hear that up in Nova Scotia, where I visited Sydney Mines, they are proposing power plants that will take advantage of the massive tides. I hope they do and I support it. I also support Jim Gordon and his wind farm. There is no place apart.

9. **READD** ▶ As you read lines 112–133, continue to cite textual evidence.
- Underline the conclusions that Gessner reaches about turbines on Cape Cod.
- Circle text that discusses bird fatalities.

10. ◀ **REREAD** . Reread lines 112–133. How does Gessner react to the "statistic" about wind farms and the Gulf oil spill? Why does he include this interaction in the piece?

_____

_____

_____

_____

_____

_____

_____

SHORT RESPONSE

Cite Text Evidence In what ways does the structure of Gessner's essay help engage his reader? **Cite text evidence** in your response.

_____

_____

_____

_____

_____

_____

_____

_____

_____

_____

A New Birth of Freedom

A New Birth of Freedom

"My father was a slave and my people died to build this country, and I'm going to stay here and have a part of it."

—Paul Robeson

© Houghton Mifflin Harcourt Publishing Company • Image Credits: Library of Congress Prints and Photographs Division Washington, D.C.

Background Abraham Lincoln *(1809–1865) was elected president in 1860 and was clear in his opposition to expanding slavery to U.S. territories in the West. By the time of Lincoln's inauguration in March of 1861, seven slave states had formed the Confederacy and seceded from the Union. By April, the Union and the Confederacy were at war. After the Union victory at Antietam in September 1862, Lincoln issued a preliminary proclamation, stating that on January 1, 1863, slaves in rebel states would be declared free. Though more of a symbolic gesture than an enforceable law, the Emancipation Proclamation heartened abolitionists and African Americans and made the issue of slavery a central focus of the war.*

The Emancipation Proclamation

Legal Document by Abraham Lincoln

CLOSE READ
Notes

1. **READD** ▷ As you read lines 1–21, begin to cite text evidence.

   - Circle the three dates noted in these lines.
   - Underline the states affected by the proclamation, and in the margin explain which states this proclamation affects (lines 5–12).
   - Underline text that explains how the president will classify the states (lines 13–21).

A Transcription By the President of the United States of America: A Proclamation.

Whereas, on the twenty-second day of September, in the year of our Lord one thousand eight hundred and sixty-two, a proclamation was issued by the President of the United States, containing, among other things, the following, to wit:[1]

"That on the first day of January, in the year of our Lord one thousand eight hundred and sixty-three, all persons held as slaves within any State or designated part of a State, the people whereof shall then be in rebellion against the United States, shall be then, thenceforward, and forever free; and the Executive Government of the United States, including the military and naval

10 authority thereof, will recognize and maintain the freedom of such persons, and will do no act or acts to repress such persons, or any of them, in any efforts they may make for their actual freedom.

---

[1] **to wit:** namely.

CLOSE READ Notes

"That the Executive will, on the first day of January aforesaid,[2] by proclamation, designate the States and parts of States, if any, in which the people thereof, respectively, shall then be in rebellion against the United States; and the fact that any State, or the people thereof, shall on that day be, in good faith, represented in the Congress of the United States by members chosen thereto at elections wherein a majority of the qualified voters of such State shall have participated, shall, in the absence of strong countervailing[3] testimony, be

20   deemed conclusive evidence that such State, and the people thereof, are not then in rebellion against the United States."

Now, therefore I, Abraham Lincoln, President of the United States, by virtue of the power in me vested as Commander-in-Chief, of the Army and Navy of the United States in time of actual armed rebellion against the authority and government of the United States, and as a fit and necessary war measure for **suppressing** said rebellion, do, on this first day of January, in the year of our Lord one thousand eight hundred and sixty-three, and in accordance with my purpose so to do publicly proclaimed for the full period of one hundred days, from the day first above mentioned, order and designate as

30   the States and parts of States wherein the people thereof respectively, are this day in rebellion against the United States, the following, to wit:

suppressing:

---

[2] **aforesaid:** stated before.
[3] **countervailing:** contradicting.

2. ◀ REREAD Reread lines 13–21. What is Lincoln's purpose in this paragraph and how does he achieve it? Cite text evidence in your response.

_____

_____

_____

_____

_____

3. READ ▶ As you read lines 22–40, continue to cite text evidence.

- Circle the authority by which Lincoln makes the January 1, 1863, proclamation.
- Underline the reason Lincoln gives for making the proclamation.
- In the margin of lines 32–40, explain the reason for the exceptions.

58

© Houghton Mifflin Harcourt Publishing Company

Arkansas, Texas, Louisiana, (except the Parishes of St. Bernard, Plaquemines, Jefferson, St. John, St. Charles, St. James Ascension, Assumption, Terrebonne, Lafourche, St. Mary, St. Martin, and Orleans, including the City of New Orleans) Mississippi, Alabama, Florida, Georgia, South Carolina, North Carolina, and Virginia, (except the forty-eight counties designated as West Virginia, and also the counties of Berkley, Accomac, Northampton, Elizabeth City, York, Princess Ann, and Norfolk, including the cities of Norfolk and Portsmouth), and which excepted parts, are for the present, left precisely as if
40 this proclamation were not issued.

And by virtue of the power, and for the purpose aforesaid, I do order and declare that all persons held as slaves within said designated States, and parts of States, are, and henceforward shall be free; and that the Executive government of the United States, including the military and naval authorities thereof, will recognize and maintain the freedom of said persons.

And I hereby enjoin upon[4] the people so declared to be free to abstain from all violence, unless in necessary self-defence; and I recommend to them that, in all cases when allowed, they labor faithfully for reasonable wages.

And I further declare and make known, that such persons of suitable
50 condition, will be received into the armed service of the United States to **garrison** forts, positions, stations, and other places, and to man vessels of all sorts in said service.

garrison:

_____

[4] **enjoin upon:** direct.

---

4. ◀ **REREAD** Reread lines 22–31. Interpret the meaning of "the full period of one hundred days." Cite text evidence in your answer.

_____

_____

_____

_____

_____

5. **READ** ▷ As you read lines 41–60, continue to cite text evidence.

• In the margin, explain Lincoln's order and declaration (lines 41–45).
• Underline parts of Lincoln's message that are directed to newly freed people.
• Circle reasons Lincoln offers to support his argument that this proclamation is justified.

© Houghton Mifflin Harcourt Publishing Company

invoke:

And upon this act, sincerely believed to be an act of justice, warranted by the Constitution, upon military necessity, I **invoke** the considerate judgment of mankind, and the gracious favor of Almighty God.

In witness whereof, I have hereunto set my hand and caused the seal of the United States to be affixed.

Done at the City of Washington, this first day of January, in the year of our Lord one thousand eight hundred and sixty three, and of the Independence of
60   the United States of America the eighty-seventh.

By the President: ABRAHAM LINCOLN
WILLIAM H. SEWARD, Secretary of State.

6.   **◀ REREAD AND DISCUSS**   Reread lines 41–60. With a small group, discuss the purpose of these lines. What do you think Lincoln envisioned would happen as a result of this proclamation?

SHORT RESPONSE

Cite Text Evidence   Analyze Lincoln's argument that he is taking action that is of "military necessity." Refer to your reading notes, and **cite text evidence** in your response.

_____

_____

_____

_____

_____

_____

_____

© Houghton Mifflin Harcourt Publishing Company • Image Credits: ©Todd Gipstein/National Geographic/Getty Images

Background *The Iroquois Confederacy, also known as the League of Five Nations, was a union of five American Indian tribes across upper New York State. Around 1570, so the legend goes, a visionary named* **Dekanawida** *convinced the nations to unite in order to establish peace. The Iroquois Constitution is regarded as the world's oldest living constitution. In 1988, to mark the bicentennial of the U.S. Constitution, Congress passed a resolution stating that "the confederation of the original Thirteen Colonies into one republic was influenced by the political system developed by the Iroquois Confederacy, as were many of the democratic principles which were incorporated into the Constitution itself."*

from The Iroquois Constitution

Public Document by Dekanawida

CLOSE READ
Notes

1. **READD** ▶ As you read lines 1–24, begin to collect and cite text evidence.

   • Circle the author's name and his purpose in the first sentence.

   • In the margin, explain what Dekanawida does first.

   • Read the footnotes. In the margin, hypothesize the reason Dekanawida first addresses Adodarhoh.

Tree of Great Peace

I am Dekanawida[1] and with the Five Nations' Confederate Lords I plant the Tree of the Great Peace. I plant it in your territory, Adodarhoh,[2] and the Onondaga Nation, in the territory of you who are Firekeepers.

I name the tree the Tree of the Great Long Leaves. Under the shade of this Tree of the Great Peace we spread the soft white feathery down of the globe thistle as seats for you, Adodarhoh, and your cousin Lords.

We place you upon those seats, spread soft with the feathery down of the globe thistle, there beneath the shade of the spreading branches of the Tree of Peace. There shall you sit and watch the Council Fire of the Confederacy of the Five Nations, and all the affairs of the Five Nations shall be transacted at this place before you, Adodarhoh, and your cousin Lords, by the Confederate Lords of the Five Nations.

10

---

[1] **Dekanawida:** the legendary Great Peacemaker.
[2] **Adodarhoh:** the Onondaga Chief who was the last to join the peace pact.

© Houghton Mifflin Harcourt Publishing Company • Image Credits: ©Erwin Sherman

Roots have spread out from the Tree of the Great Peace, one to the north, one to the east, one to the south, and one to the west. The name of these roots is The Great White Roots and their nature is Peace and Strength.

If any man or any nation outside the Five Nations shall obey the laws of the Great Peace and make known their **disposition** to the Lords of the Confederacy, they may trace the Roots to the Tree and if their minds are clean and they are obedient and promise to obey the wishes of the Confederate

20   Council, they shall be welcomed to take shelter beneath the Tree of the Long Leaves.

We place at the top of the Tree of the Long Leaves an Eagle who is able to see afar. If he sees in the distance any evil approaching or any danger threatening he will at once warn the people of the Confederacy.

Leaders

The Lords of the Confederacy of the Five Nations shall be mentors of the people for all time. The thickness of their skin shall be seven spans—which is to say that they shall be proof against anger, offensive actions, and criticism. Their hearts shall be full of peace and goodwill and their minds filled with a yearning for the welfare of the people of the Confederacy. With endless

30   patience they shall carry out their duty and their firmness shall be tempered with a tenderness for their people. Neither anger nor fury shall find lodgment in their minds and all their words and actions shall be marked by calm deliberation.

disposition:

2. **◀ REREAD** Reread lines 1–24. What do you think was the author's purpose in using tree roots as the symbol for the Iroquois Confederacy? Cite text evidence to support your answer.

_____

_____

_____

_____

3. **READ ▶** As you read lines 25–48, continue to cite text evidence.

- Underline language describing the leaders of the Confederacy of the Five Nations.
- In the margin, explain the special role given to women (lines 34–36).
- Circle text explaining the symbolism of the five arrows.

© Houghton Mifflin Harcourt Publishing Company

© Houghton Mifflin Harcourt Publishing Company • Image Credits: ©Colin D. Young/Shutterstock

Clans

The lineal descent[3] of the people of the Five Nations shall run in the female line. Women shall be considered the **progenitors** of the Nation. They shall own the land and the soil. Men and women shall follow the status of the mother.

progenitors:

Symbols

Five arrows shall be bound together very strong and each arrow shall represent one nation. As the five arrows are strongly bound this shall symbolize the complete union of the nations. Thus are the Five Nations united
40   completely and enfolded together, united into one head, one body, and one mind. Therefore they shall labor, legislate, and council together for the interest of future generations.

War and Peace

I, Dekanawida, and the Union Lords, now uproot the tallest pine tree and into the cavity thereby made we cast all weapons of war. Into the depths of the earth, down into the deep underearth currents of water flowing to unknown regions we cast all the weapons of strife. We bury them from sight and we plant again the tree. Thus shall the Great Peace be established and hostilities shall no longer be known between the Five Nations but peace to the United People.

---

[3] **lineal descent:** line of ancestors.

4. (◀ **REREAD**) Reread lines 43–48. What is the symbolic meaning of burying the weapons of war deep in the earth? How do the pine tree and the currents of water add to this symbol? Cite text evidence in your response.

_____

_____

_____

_____

_____

_____

_____

SHORT RESPONSE

Cite Text Evidence   What is Dekanawida's primary purpose for writing this constitution? What steps does he take to make sure the Confederacy is successful? Refer to your reading notes, and be sure to **cite text evidence** in your response.

_____

_____

_____

_____

_____

_____

_____

_____

_____

© Houghton Mifflin Harcourt Publishing Company

© Houghton Mifflin Harcourt Publishing Company • Image Credits: ©Cal Sport Media via AP Images

Background *In 2005, the National Collegiate Athletic Association (N.C.A.A.) banned the use of American Indian mascots by sports teams during their postseason tournaments. At least eighteen schools had mascots that the N.C.A.A. deemed "hostile or abusive." Almost immediately, protests arose, especially from Florida State University, home of the Florida Seminoles. Read the article below to find out what stirred the controversy and the result of the N.C.A.A. decision.*

Bonding Over a Mascot

Newspaper Article by Joe Lapointe

CLOSE READ
Notes

1. **READD ▷** As you read lines 1–25, begin to collect and cite evidence.

   - Circle text that describes the relationship between the Seminoles and Florida State University.
   - Underline how Toni Sanchez feels about the university's American Indian statue and the N.C.A.A. policy.
   - In the margin, explain the N.C.A.A "crackdown."

December 29, 2006

A few new statues of a Seminole family in 19th-century clothing stand outside the football stadium at Florida State University. The father holds a long gun, the son a bow and arrow, and the mother an infant in her arms as she looks warily to her right.

The statues represent the era when the Seminoles and the United States were at war. The public art is part of a complex relationship between Seminole culture and sports at Florida State. This bond has strengthened since a crackdown by the National Collegiate Athletic Association last year against American Indian mascots, nicknames and imagery among sports teams.

10 Not every university enjoys a harmonious relationship with Indians. But a sense of cooperation seems to **permeate** the Florida State campus in Tallahassee, Fla., where Toni Sanchez was among 21 students to complete a new course this month called History of the Seminoles and Southeastern Tribes.

permeate:

edict:

Sanchez, a senior majoring in English, called the N.C.A.A. **edict** "beyond idiotic" and offensive. She described the new statues as beautiful.

"I know what a real Seminole is," she said. "This Anglo guilt and regret don't affect me."

20 Sanchez is from a family with Seminole and Hispanic ancestry. Her father, once a farm worker, is now a casino operator. Her mother is a teacher. Sanchez also plays trumpet at football games in a marching band that wears arrowheads on the back of its uniforms.

Of the tribal flag near the new statues, another recent addition, she said, "Every time I look at it, I get really giddy inside." Of the use of the Seminole imagery for the university's sports, she said, "I'm so proud of it."

Florida State was one of 18 institutions cited by the N.C.A.A. in August 2005 for "mascots, nicknames or images deemed hostile or abusive in terms of race, ethnicity or national origin." The institutions were forbidden to use the symbols in postseason events controlled by the N.C.A.A., like the national 30 championship basketball tournament that begins in March.

Five programs have since received permission to continue using their imagery because they received approval from specific Indian groups, in Florida State's case the 3,200-member Seminole Tribe of Florida. Five others have changed or are in the process of changing, said Bob Williams, an N.C.A.A. spokesman. The other eight, he said, remain on the list and are subject to the policy, including the Illinois Fighting Illini and the North Dakota Fighting Sioux.

Myles Brand, the president of the N.C.A.A., said in a telephone interview last week that his organization made the right decision but witnessed more 40 negative reaction to the ruling than expected.

"What we've accomplished in part is to raise the level of awareness nationally about how we treat Native Americans," Brand said. "If we don't stand by our values, we lose our integrity."

caricature:

At times, Indians are reduced to casual **caricature** that would not be tolerated by other groups, he said, adding that the N.C.A.A. had been honored for its stance by Indian groups in Oklahoma and Indiana.

---

2. **◀ REREAD** Reread lines 15–18. What does Sanchez imply is the real reason behind the N.C.A.A ban? Cite textual evidence.

_____

_____

3. **READ ▶** As you read lines 26–51, circle text from the N.C.A.A.'s statement. Then, underline the opinions of Brand and Wetherell.

© Houghton Mifflin Harcourt Publishing Company

Less complimentary is T. K. Wetherell, the president of Florida State, who said the N.C.A.A. was "more interested in being politically correct" and did not consult the Seminole tribe before making its decision.

50 "The way they weaseled out was to say, 'O.K., as long as the tribe continues to support it,'" he said.

Wetherell, a former Florida State football player who also teaches history, wore a hunting outfit when interviewed recently in his office. He pointed to a team logo of an Indian's face that he said had elements of caricature. "That's not really a Seminole-looking deal," Wetherell said. "This is a marketing tool." He said the university might "gradually let certain things fade."

He said he told the Seminole Tribe of Florida's council, "If you don't want Florida State to be the Seminoles, we ain't Seminoles anymore." Wetherell said the tribe approved the use partly because the campus is in the capital and tribal 60 leaders "are not only good businessmen, they are great politicians."

He said the new history course was proposed before the N.C.A.A. edict.

But Neil Jumonville, the chairman of the history department, said the N.C.A.A. resolution accelerated the creation of the class and that his staff received advice from local Seminole leaders.

4. **◀ REREAD** Reread lines 38–51. Explain the conflict between Brand and Wetherell.

_____

_____

_____

_____

_____

5. **READ ▶** As you read lines 52–81, continue to cite text evidence.

- Write in the margin what you can infer about Wetherell's comments about the team logo.
- Underline text explaining why the university keeps the mascot and why the Seminole tribe didn't fight to have it changed.
- Circle what Versen hopes the students will explore in the class.

© Houghton Mifflin Harcourt Publishing Company

"These are people who are savvy about their place in the American myth," Jumonville said. "And they are smart enough to manipulate the myth for their own good."

The first class was taught by Christopher R. Versen, who recently earned his doctorate in American history.

70   "I wanted to challenge students to think about identity," Versen said. "What is it inside us that makes us identify ourselves one way or another? What external factors play into identity?"

amalgam:

The Seminoles are an **amalgam** of several tribes, predominantly Creek, that included escaped slaves. They migrated south to the Everglades in retreat from the United States Army. Some were driven out during the Trail of Tears[1] period under President Andrew Jackson.

Those descendants live as the Seminole Nation of Oklahoma. The Seminoles in Florida once had a commercial hunting economy. Since 1979, their economic status has improved because of casino gambling.

80   Earlier this month, the Seminoles acquired Hard Rock International—the music-themed chain of restaurants, hotels and casinos—for $965 million.

Versen said he did not discuss sports identity with his students because he was afraid it would become a distraction. But a guest speaker who raised the mascot issue was Max Osceola, one of three councilmen for the Seminole Tribe of Florida.

---

[1] **Trail of Tears:** In 1838 and 1839, Jackson's policy forced the Cherokee nation to leave their home east of the Mississippi River and relocate to present-day Oklahoma. Over 4,000 people lost their lives to hunger, disease, and exhaustion during the march.

6. **◀ REREAD** Reread lines 52–81. Why does Lapointe include information about the Seminoles' history and their situation today?

_____

_____

_____

_____

7. **READ ▶** As you read lines 82–118, continue to cite evidence.

• Circle the description of Max Osceola in lines 82–90. Circle his description of the old Sammy Seminole.

• Underline the description of the new mascot.

• In the margin, explain Max Osceola's point of view.

© Houghton Mifflin Harcourt Publishing Company

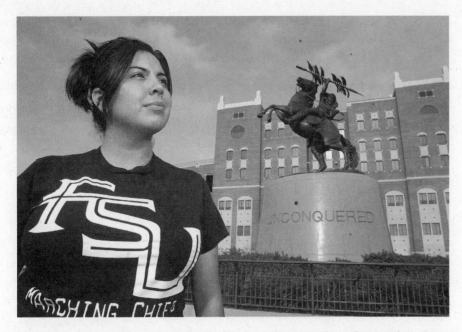

Toni Sanchez, a student who is from a family with Seminole and Hispanic ancestry, is proud of the use of Seminole imagery at Florida State.

"If I had a child and named it after you, would you consider it an honor?" Osceola said he asked the students. He also reflected on a former mascot, Sammy Seminole, who was retired in 1972.

"He had a big nose and he lived in a teepee," Osceola said. "He looked like a buffoon."

90

The current mascot is named, coincidentally, Osceola, after a 19th-century warrior. A student dressed as Osceola rides a horse named Renegade onto the football field and throws a flaming spear. This mascot's clothing was designed by the tribe.

Tina Osceola, who is the executive director of the tribe's historical resources department and is a cousin of Max Osceola's, said, "We've given them license to be theatrical."

A statue of the warrior riding atop Renegade stands outside the stadium above the word "Unconquered," because the Seminoles never surrendered to the United States.

100

When the Seminoles announced in New York the purchase of Hard Rock, Max Osceola joked that Indians once sold Manhattan for trinkets but were now "going to buy Manhattan back, one burger at a time."

Not everyone outside the tribe approves of all of the Indian trappings at sporting events, including the tomahawk chop hand gesture and a droning cheer that sounds like background music heard in old western movies.

Joe Quetone, the executive director of the nonprofit Florida Governor's Council on Indian Affairs Inc., said, "Things fans do are outrageous and ridiculous."

110   Bobby Bowden, the head football coach, did not respond to four recent requests for comment on the issue placed with the university's sports information department.

From a student's perspective, Sanchez said that people who were genuinely concerned with the circumstances of Indians should concentrate less on sports iconography and more on alcoholism, suicide, teen pregnancy and high school dropout rates.

"After all those years of diseases, occupation and war, we're still here," she said. "I refuse to believe that a silly mascot will take us down."

8. **◀ REREAD** Reread lines 82–118. What does Sanchez mean when she says that a mascot won't "take us down"?

_____

_____

_____

SHORT RESPONSE

Cite Text Evidence What is the author's purpose in writing this newspaper article? **Cite text evidence** to show how he supports his ideas in your response.

_____

_____

_____

_____

_____

_____

_____

_____

© Houghton Mifflin Harcourt Publishing Company

© Houghton Mifflin Harcourt Publishing Company ∘ Image Credits: ©Nick Norman/National Geographic/Getty Images

An Age of Realism

An Age of Realism

"Reality is that which, when you stop believing in it, doesn't go away."

—Phillip K. Dick

SHORT STORY
The Men in the Storm   **Stephen Crane**

SCIENCE WRITING
The Yuckiest Food in the Amazon   **Mary Roach**

SHORT STORY
A Journey   **Edith Wharton**

POEM
Ode to a Large Tuna
in the Market   **Pablo Neruda**

© Houghton Mifflin Harcourt Publishing Company ○ Image Credits: ©Nick Norman/National Geographic/Getty Images

Background Stephen Crane *(1871–1900)—American novelist, poet, and short story writer—was one of the most innovative writers of his generation, known for his gritty realism and willingness to take on difficult themes such as fear, social isolation, and spiritual crisis. He is perhaps best known for his Civil War novel* The Red Badge of Courage *(1895), which depicts the psychological complexities of the battlefield. Crane, who dropped out of college and moved to New York to be a writer, had an adventurous life that was tragically cut short when he died of tuberculosis at the age of 28. Crane's work was nearly forgotten until two decades later when it was "rediscovered" by critics.*

The Men in the Storm

Short Story by Stephen Crane

CLOSE READ
Notes

1. (**READ** ▶) As you read lines 1–27, begin to collect and cite text evidence.

- Underline images that help you visualize the weather.
- Circle images of street life.
- In the margin, describe the setting (lines 1–13).

At about three o'clock of the February afternoon, the blizzard began to
swirl great clouds of snow along the streets, sweeping it down from the
roofs and up from the pavements until the faces of pedestrians tingled and
burned as from a thousand needle-prickings. Those on the walks huddled their
necks closely in the collars of their coats and went along stooping like a race of
aged people. The drivers of vehicles hurried their horses furiously on their way.
They were made more cruel by the exposure of their positions, aloft on high
seats. The street cars, bound up-town, went slowly, the horses slipping and
straining in the spongy brown mass that lay between the rails. The drivers,
10   muffled to the eyes, stood erect and facing the wind, models of grim
philosophy. Overhead the trains rumbled and roared, and the dark structure of
the elevated railroad, stretching over the avenue, dripped little streams and
drops of water upon the mud and snow beneath it.

© Houghton Mifflin Harcourt Publishing Company • Image Credits: ©Bettmann/Corbis; ©PhotoLink/Photodisc/Getty Images

All the clatter of the street was softened by the masses that lay upon the cobbles until, even to one who looked from a window, it became important music, a melody of life made necessary to the ear by the dreariness of the pitiless beat and sweep of the storm. Occasionally one could see black figures of men busily shovelling the white drifts from the walks. The sounds from their labor created new recollections of rural experiences which every man manages

20 to have in a measure. Later, the immense windows of the shops became aglow with light, throwing great beams of orange and yellow upon the pavement. They were infinitely cheerful, yet in a way they accented the force and discomfort of the storm, and gave a meaning to the pace of the people and the vehicles, scores of pedestrians and drivers, wretched with cold faces, necks and feet, speeding for scores of unknown doors and entrances, scattering to an infinite variety of shelters, to places which the imagination made warm with the familiar colors of home.

There was an absolute expression of hot dinners in the pace of the people. If one dared to speculate upon the destination of those who came trooping, he

30 lost himself in a maze of social calculations; he might fling a handful of sand and attempt to follow the flight of each particular grain. But as to the suggestion of hot dinners, he was in firm lines of thought, for it was upon every hurrying face. It is a matter of tradition; it is from the tales of childhood. It comes forth with every storm.

---

2. (◀ REREAD) Reread lines 1–27. Describe the contrast between the storm outside and the people who remain inside. Cite evidence from the text.

_____

_____

_____

_____

_____

_____

3. (READ ▶) As you read lines 28–61, continue to cite textual evidence.

• In the margin, explain what is on everyone's mind.
• Underline examples of people moving toward their destination.
• Circle descriptions of men waiting near the "charitable house."

© Houghton Mifflin Harcourt Publishing Company

However, in a certain part of a dark West-side street, there was a collection of men to whom these things were as if they were not. In this street was located a charitable house where for five cents the homeless of the city could get a bed at night and, in the morning, coffee and bread.

During the afternoon of the storm, the whirling snows acted as drivers, as men with whips, and at half-past three, the walk before the closed doors of the house was covered with wanderers of the street, waiting. For some distance on either side of the place they could be seen lurking in doorways and behind projecting parts of buildings, gathering in close bunches in an effort to get warm. A covered wagon drawn up near the curb sheltered a dozen of them. Under the stairs that led to the elevated railway station, there were six or eight, their hands stuffed deep in their pockets, their shoulders stooped, jiggling their feet. Others always could be seen coming, a strange procession, some slouching along with the characteristic hopeless gait of professional strays, some coming with hesitating steps wearing the air of men to whom this sort of thing was new.

---

4. **◀ REREAD** Reread lines 39–55. How is the situation getting worse for the men? Cite textual evidence in your response.

_____

_____

_____

_____

_____

_____

© Houghton Mifflin Harcourt Publishing Company • Image Credits: ©Everett Collection Historical/Alamy

It was an afternoon of incredible length. The snow, blowing in twisting clouds, sought out the men in their meagre hiding-places and skilfully beat in among them, drenching their persons with showers of fine, stinging flakes. They crowded together, muttering, and fumbling in their pockets to get their red, inflamed wrists covered by the cloth.

Newcomers usually halted at one of the groups and addressed a question, perhaps much as a matter of form, "Is it open yet?"

Those who had been waiting inclined to take the questioner seriously and become contemptuous. "No; do yeh think we'd be standin' here?"

60 The gathering swelled in numbers steadily and persistently. One could always see them coming, trudging slowly through the storm.

Finally, the little snow plains in the street began to assume a leaden hue from the shadows of evening. The buildings upreared gloomily save where various windows became brilliant figures of light that made shimmers and splashes of yellow on the snow. A street lamp on the curb struggled to illuminate, but it was reduced to impotent blindness by the swift gusts of sleet crusting its panes.

In this half-darkness, the men began to come from their shelter places and mass in front of the doors of charity. They were of all types, but the

70 nationalities were mostly American, German and Irish. Many were strong, healthy, clear-skinned fellows with that stamp of countenance which is not frequently seen upon seekers after charity. There were men of undoubted patience, industry and temperance, who in time of ill-fortune, do not habitually turn to rail at the state of society, snarling at the arrogance of the rich and bemoaning the cowardice of the poor, but who at these times are apt to wear a sudden and singular meekness, as if they saw the world's progress marching from them and were trying to perceive where they had failed, what they had lacked, to be thus vanquished in the race. Then there were others of

5. **READ ▶** As you read lines 62–125, continue to cite textual evidence.

- Underline the descriptions of the "men of industry."
- In the margin, summarize the essential difference between the "men of industry" and the "Bowery lodging-house element."
- Circle the lines that describe the problem the men face, and explain the problem in the margin (lines 107–115).

© Houghton Mifflin Harcourt Publishing Company

80 the shifting, Bowery lodging-house element who were used to paying ten cents
for a place to sleep, but who now came here because it was cheaper.

But they were all mixed in one mass so thoroughly that one could not have
discerned the different elements but for the fact that the laboring men, for the
most part, remained silent and impassive in the blizzard, their eyes fixed on
the windows of the house, statues of patience.

The sidewalk soon became completely blocked by the bodies of the men.
They pressed close to one another like sheep in a winter's gale, keeping one
another warm by the heat of their bodies. The snow came down upon this
compressed group of men until, directly from above, it might have appeared
like a heap of snow-covered merchandise, if it were not for the fact that the

90 crowd swayed gently with a unanimous, rhythmical motion. It was wonderful
to see how the snow lay upon the heads and shoulders of these men, in little
ridges an inch thick perhaps in places, the flakes steadily adding drop and
drop, precisely as they fall upon the unresisting grass of the fields. The feet of
the men were all wet and cold and the wish to warm them accounted for the
slow, gentle, rhythmical motion. Occasionally some man whose ears or nose
tingled acutely from the cold winds would wriggle down until his head was
protected by the shoulders of his companions.

There was a continuous murmuring discussion as to the probability of the
doors being speedily opened. They persistently lifted their eyes toward the

100 windows. One could hear little combats of opinion.

"There's a light in th' winder!"

"Naw; it's a reflection f'm across th' way."

"Well, didn't I see 'em lite it?"

"You did?"

"I did!"

"Well, then, that settles it!"

As the time approached when they expected to be allowed to enter, the
men crowded to the doors in an unspeakable crush, jamming and wedging in a
way that it seemed would crack bones. They surged heavily against the building

110 in a powerful wave of pushing shoulders. Once a rumor flitted among all the
tossing heads.

"They can't open th' doors! Th' fellers er smack up ag'in 'em."

Then a dull roar of rage came from the men on the outskirts; but all the
time they strained and pushed until it appeared to be impossible for those that
they cried out against to do anything but be crushed to pulp.

"Ah, git away f'm th' door!"

"Git outa that!"

"Throw 'em out!"

"Kill 'em!"

120   "Say, fellers, now, what th' 'ell? Give 'em a chanct t' open th' door!"

"Yeh damned pigs, give 'em a chanct t' open th' door!"

Men in the outskirts of the crowd occasionally yelled when a boot-heel of one of frantic trampling feet crushed on their freezing extremities.

"Git off me feet, yeh clumsy tarrier!"

"Say, don't stand on me feet! Walk on th' ground!"

A man near the doors suddenly shouted: "O-o-oh! Le' me out—le' me out!" And another, a man of infinite valor, once twisted his head so as to half face those who were pushing behind him. "Quit yer shovin', yeh"—and he delivered a volley of the most powerful and singular **invective** straight into the faces of

invective:

130   the men behind him. It was as if he was hammering the noses of them with curses of triple brass. His face, red with rage, could be seen; upon it, an expression of sublime disregard of consequences. But nobody cared to reply to his imprecations; it was too cold. Many of them snickered and all continued to push.

6. ◀ **REREAD** Reread lines 101–125. How does the author's use of dialect affect the story?

_____

_____

_____

_____

_____

_____

7. **READ** ▶ As you read lines 126–174, continue to cite textual evidence.

- Underline details that describe the conditions outside.
- Circle details that describe the man in the window across the street.
- In the margin, explain the reactions of the men to the man in the dry goods store.

> **But nobody cared to reply to his imprecations; it was too cold.**

In occasional pauses of the crowd's movement the men had opportunity to make jokes; usually grim things, and no doubt very uncouth. Nevertheless, they are notable—one does not expect to find the quality of humor in a heap of old clothes under a snowdrift.

The winds seemed to grow fiercer as time wore on. Some of the gusts of snow that came down on the close collection of heads cut like knives and needles, and the men huddled, and swore, not like dark assassins, but in a sort of an American fashion, grimly and desperately, it is true, but yet with a wondrous under-effect, indefinable and **mystic**, as if there was some kind of humor in this catastrophe, in this situation in a night of snow-laden winds.

Once, the window of the huge dry-goods shop across the street furnished material for a few moments of forgetfulness. In the brilliantly-lighted space appeared the figure of a man. He was rather stout and very well clothed. His whiskers were fashioned charmingly after those of the Prince of Wales. He stood in an attitude of magnificent reflection. He slowly stroked his moustache with a certain grandeur of manner, and looked down at the snow-encrusted mob. From below, there was denoted a supreme complacence in him. It seemed that the sight operated inversely, and enabled him to more clearly regard his own environment, delightful relatively.

One of the mob chanced to turn his head and perceive the figure in the window. "Hello, lookit 'is whiskers," he said genially.

Many of the men turned then, and a shout went up. They called to him in all strange keys. They addressed him in every manner, from familiar and cordial greetings to carefully-worded advice concerning changes in his personal appearance. The man presently fled, and the mob chuckled ferociously like ogres who had just devoured something.

mystic:

8. ◀ **REREAD AND DISCUSS** Reread lines 154–160. In a small group, discuss how the men show solidarity with one another.

They turned then to serious business. Often they addressed the stolid front of the house.

"Oh, let us in fer Gawd's sake!"

"Let us in or we'll all drop dead!"

"Say, what's th' use o' keepin' all us poor Indians out in th' cold?"

And always some one was saying, "Keep off me feet."

The crushing of the crowd grew terrific toward the last. The men, in keen pain from the blasts, began almost to fight. With the pitiless whirl of snow upon them, the battle for shelter was going to the strong. It became known that
170 the basement door at the foot of a little steep flight of stairs was the one to be opened, and they jostled and heaved in this direction like laboring fiends. One could hear them panting and groaning in their fierce exertion.

Usually some one in the front ranks was protesting to those in the rear: "O —o—ow! Oh, say, now, fellers, let up, will yeh? Do yeh wanta kill somebody?"

A policeman arrived and went into the midst of them, scolding and berating, occasionally threatening, but using no force but that of his hands and shoulders against these men who were only struggling to get in out of the storm. His decisive tones rang out sharply: "Stop that pushin' back there! Come, boys, don't push! Stop that! Here, you, quit yer shovin'! Cheese that!"

180 When the door below was opened, a thick stream of men forced a way down the stairs, which were of an extraordinary narrowness and seemed only wide enough for one at a time. Yet they somehow went down almost three abreast. It was a difficult and painful operation. The crowd was like a turbulent water forcing itself through one tiny outlet. The men in the rear, excited by the success of the others, made frantic exertions, for it seemed that this large band would more than fill the quarters and that many would be left upon the pavements. It would be disastrous to be of the last, and accordingly men with the snow biting their faces, writhed and twisted with their might. One expected that from the tremendous pressure, the narrow passage to the basement door

9. **READ ▶** As you read lines 175–208, continue to cite evidence.

- Underline the lines that depict the men as a force of nature.
- Circle text describing how the men change when they enter the doorway.
- In the margin, explain why those at the back of the crowd become frantic.
- Underline words that convey hopelessness in lines 204–208.

190   would be so choked and clogged with human limbs and bodies that movement would be impossible. Once indeed the crowd was forced to stop, and a cry went along that a man had been injured at the foot of the stairs. But presently the slow movement began again, and the policeman fought at the top of the flight to ease the pressure on those who were going down.

     A reddish light from a window fell upon the faces of the men when they, in turn, arrived at the last three steps and were about to enter. One could then note a change of expression that had come over their features. As they thus stood upon the threshold of their hopes, they looked suddenly content and complacent. The fire had passed from their eyes and the snarl had vanished

200   from their lips. The very force of the crowd in the rear, which had previously vexed them, was regarded from another point of view, for it now made it inevitable that they should go through the little doors into the place that was cheery and warm with light.

     The tossing crowd on the sidewalk grew smaller and smaller. The snow beat with merciless persistence upon the bowed heads of those who waited. The wind drove it up from the pavements in frantic forms of winding white, and it seethed in circles about the huddled forms, passing in, one by one, three by three, out of the storm.

10. **◀ REREAD** As you reread lines 204–208, explain what happens at the end
of the story.

_____

_____

_____

_____

_____

SHORT RESPONSE

Cite Text Evidence Identify the theme of the story and explain how its
central ideas develop, interact, and build on one another throughout the
course of the text. Be sure to support your ideas by **citing text evidence**.

_____

_____

_____

_____

_____

_____

_____

_____

_____

_____

_____

Background *What tastes worse than rodent knee and saliva-flavored manioc mash? It depends on where you come from, as writer* **Mary Roach** *learned in a remote Amazon village. In 1998, Roach accompanied anthropologist John Patton to the village of Conambo in Ecuador, where he was studying the Achuar people. Although usually up for any adventure, Roach had some hesitation when faced with the local food, as described in the following article.*

The Yuckiest Food in the Amazon

Science Writing by Mary Roach

1. **READE ▷** As you read lines 1–38, begin to collect and cite evidence.

CLOSE READ
Notes

   • Underline conclusions that Rozin learns from his research.
   • Circle examples of things Roach has eaten in her travels.
   • In the margin, explain the "huge difference" Roach describes in lines 27–32.

In 1986, a psychologist named Paul Rozin took a group of toddlers and did a peculiar thing. One by one, he sat them down at a table and presented them with a plate of what he said was dog-doo and asked them if they'd like to eat it. (In fact, it was peanut butter, scented with bleu cheese.) Then he did the same with a sterilized grasshopper. Sixty-two percent of the children under 2 happily dispatched the **ersatz** turd; 31 percent the insect. Older children invariably rejected both plates. His point: Disgust is learned. Culture is our instructor. We are taught that horse meat is disgusting but chicken embryos are not; that Slim Jims are tasty and crickets are gross.

10   **Espousing**, as I have, a belief that nothing is inherently disgusting, that it's all a case of mind over culture, I have frequently, in my travels, felt the need to put my money where my mouth is and my mouth where it would rather not go. I have eaten walrus meat left buried on an Arctic beach to "ferment" for a month, a raw fish eye and its accompanying musculature, duck tongue, caribou marrow, brain, flipper, ant. I am, yes, one of those annoying travelers who

ersatz:

espouse:

Photo by Victor Englebert/Time Life Pictures/Getty Images

boast about the disgusting food they've lived to tell about (and tell about and tell about).

Now I am getting my come-uppance. I am getting it big-time, in a small village in the Ecuadorian Amazon. I have come here to do a story on an
20 anthropologist named John Patton. Patton studies a tribe called the Achuar, notable for their skill in blowgun-making and their long-ago rivalry with the head-shrinking Chuar. (If you've seen an authentic South American shrunken head, you've probably seen an Achuar tribesman.) Patton's base is Conambo, a scatter of houses along a fast, muddy river, reachable every now and again by a four-seater missionary plane. There is no hotel, no restaurant, no store. You eat what they hunt.

I am fast coming to understand that there is a huge difference, a vast yawning canyon of difference, between tasting something deeply unappealing and living on it. Anyone, if he tries, can suppress his disgust long enough to
30 swallow a single fish eye or a mouthful of decaying walrus. Eating enough of this sort of thing to live on is altogether a different matter. I am here for five days. I'm not doing very well.

My problem at the moment is a knee. It's a rodent knee, quietly genuflecting in a bowl of oily broth. Earlier today, the knee was attached to a

gambol:

happy, hairy, spaniel-sized rodent, **gamboling** and cavorting in the wee hours of the rain forest morning until our host happened along and plugged it full of buckshot. (Blowguns are used only on birds and pack animals like monkeys, which would be scared off by gunshot.)

The knee is one of nature's marvels, a busy intersection of tendon, bone
40 and cartilage. Be that as it may, "marvel" does not exactly describe my state of

2. ◀ **REREAD** Reread lines 10–38. Describe the tone Roach uses as she writes about "yucky" foods. Cite examples from the text.

_____

_____

_____

_____

_____

3. **READ** ▶ As you read lines 39–80, continue to cite evidence.

- Underline examples of Roach's humorous tone.
- In the margin, make an inference about why Roach must "clean my plate."
- Circle text that describes how Patton feels about his soup.

mind at the moment. Extreme psychic discomfort comes closer. The hunter and the chef are sitting directly across from me. Their generosity is heartbreaking. I have to clean my plate. I must force apart the gristly abomination with my teeth, work my tongue into its fissures and slimy orifices, extract anything vaguely chewable, and swallow it. I lean over to scout the contents of Patton's bowl.

He got the ankle. The thing about ankle bones, as schoolchildren everywhere know, is that they're attached to foot bones. And foot bones are attached to toe bones and toenails and those filthy little rubbery pads on the
50 bottom of the foot. No matter how good a meat may taste, the experience is **indelibly** marred by the act of spitting ghastly unchewables out into your fingers.

indelibly:

Patton is undaunted. He has the entire thing in his mouth. He stops sucking and gumming long enough to say: "The foot pads are a good source of fat." He is enjoying his rodent soup in the way that only a man who has been served steamed tapir[1] fetus and live palm beetles can. A hail of tiny foot bones accumulates on the ground beside him.

The knee awaits. I've finished my broth. To stall any longer would betray my revulsion. I manage to locate a couple of pockets of reasonably normal-
60 looking flesh. My inclination is to chew these slowly, forever if need be, until my hosts tire of sitting here and go off to tend the manioc[2] garden. The problem with this tactic is that boiled rodent flesh isn't the sort of thing you want to have hanging around your tongue for any longer than is strictly necessary for purposes of not choking to death. It's not really that bad, it's just strong. As in overpowering, as in taste buds passing out and waving white flags. It doesn't, in short, taste anything like chicken. I find myself chewing with my mouth open, hoping my hosts will take this for an endearing cultural peculiarity, rather than an attempt to bypass the tasting portion of my meal.

---

[1] **tapir:** a mammal related to the horse and the rhinoceros, with a flexible snout.
[2] **manioc:** a shrubby tropical plant, also known as cassava.

---

4. **◀ REREAD** Reread lines 53–57. Why does Patton seem "undaunted" about eating his rodent soup?

_____

_____

_____

_____

85

I beg Patton to take my meat. (Our hosts speak no English.) Kind soul that
70 he is, he relieves me of the knee. The man of the house makes a comment,
which Patton translates: "She doesn't like to eat?" He has seen Westerners who
don't have any children, who don't know how to shoot a rifle. Perhaps there are
Westerners who don't like eating. "She had a big breakfast," fibs Patton.

It was in fact a big breakfast, but I didn't do very much having. Someone
shot an alligator, and I had some leg. (It's a leg sort of day.) I have eaten alligator
meat before, in Florida, but someone, bless him, had taken it upon himself to
remove the scales before cooking it. (See "ghastly unchewables," above.) I tried
to pretend that the leg was something else, something bland and comforting.
After several false starts—Melba toast? lettuce?—my brain, clearly shaken,
80 presented me with "orange roughy."[3]

Patton maintains that the bulk of an Achuar's daily calories do not come
from meat. They come from *chicha*, a mildly alcoholic, vaguely nutritious,
watered-down manioc mash. Achuar men drink up to four gallons a day. If you
like chicha, you can live well in Conambo. In about an hour, I will get to try it.
Patton's friend Isaac is hosting a *minga*, a work party for the villagers who
helped Isaac's family dig a new manioc plot. It's similar in concept to the
Amish barn-raising, with marathon chicha-drinking taking the place of
square-dancing.

I am of two minds about chicha. On the one hand, it's a beverage. In the
90 land of scary food, the beverage is your friend.

On the other hand. We are talking about a beverage fermented with
human saliva. Achuar women chew boiled manioc into the desired mashed-
potato texture, and then spit-spray the contents of their bulging cheeks out into
the chicha urn. While I know that, percentage-wise, we're talking a tiny
fraction of the mixture, I'm having difficulty embracing the idea. I have a little
agreement with myself: When spittle finds its way onto the ingredient list, I
find a way to say no.

---

[3] **orange roughy:** a large, deep-sea fish native to New Zealand, also known as slimehead.

---

5. **READ ▶** As you read lines 81–135, continue to cite text evidence.

- In the margin, explain why Roach is "of two minds about chicha" (lines 89–97).
- Underline facts you learn about the etiquette of chicha making and
  consumption.
- In the margin of lines 100–108, make an inference about why Roach includes
  the description of Isaac's living room.

Indians in Ecuador cook manioc to make chicha.

"You can't say no," says Patton, tossing ankle carcass to a cringing, harelipped dog. "It's just not done."

Patton and I are seated on a low log bench in the open-walled platform that serves as Isaac's living room. The man of the house whittles blowgun darts as he chats. A pair of black horn-rim glasses sits askew on his face. One lens is violently cracked, as though someone stepped on it, though no one here has the kind of shoes for that. The floor is dirty but uncluttered. Decor runs to parrot feathers and jaguar skulls, a government poster urging vaccinations for children. In the corner, a little girl has set up a chicha tea party with her dolls, the tenderness of the scene marred only by the knowledge that the tiny chicha bowls are made from howler monkey voice boxes.

Isaac's wife and mother are in constant motion, serving bowls of chicha to the 10 or so guests. Chicha is the backbone of Achuar society. As with the ankle bone and the knee bone, you feel an unalterable pressure to accept. Chicha is

the holy communion, the Manischewitz,[4] the kava-kava[5] of Achuar life. It's
present at every ceremony, every visit, every meal. An Achuar woman's
desirability rests in no small part on her skill at chicha brewing and serving.

Isaac's mother dips a clay bowl into an urn of eggnog-hued liquid.
Something slimy dangles off the bottom of the bowl, waving howdy-doo as she
crosses the floor to our bench. Her hand is coated with a mucilaginous[6] yellow
fluid with flecks of manioc fiber. The sidewalk outside a frat house on a Sunday
morning comes, unbidden and unwelcome, to mind.

120 "It's Miller time," says Patton as he takes the bowl. After 10 minutes, he
warns, she'll return to take the bowl away and give it to someone else, most
likely me. It is considered irretrievably rude to refuse a bowl of chicha, or even
to set it down. (In a maddening instance of form following etiquette, the
ceramic bowls in which chicha is served are rounded on the bottom, so that the
drinker cannot set one down without spilling the contents.)

A refusal is interpreted as a bluff and triggers a ritualized pas de deux:[7]
"No, really, I shouldn't." "Yes, yes, I insist." Woe unto the visitor: The host
never backs down.

Which means I have 10 minutes to talk myself out of the revulsion that's
130 building in my gut, jostling for space among the pinworms and protozoa. My
mouth is full of saliva anyway, I tell myself. What's a little more? Myself isn't
buying it. Myself is noting the vast and unsettling difference between oral
hygiene practices around the Amazon basin and around the basin in our
bathroom at home. This isn't a matter of disgust, I tell Patton. It's a matter of
gum disease.

Patton wipes manioc slime from his beard. Intelligent chicha drinkers, he
holds, don't fret about the saliva it's made with. They fret about the giardia[8] and

---

[4] **Manischewitz:** a popular brand of kosher products.

[5] **kava-kava:** a ceremonial drink used in the Pacific Islands, made up of chewed or ground
pulp and cold water.

[6] **mucilaginous:** moist and sticky.

[7] **pas de deux:** a dance for two people.

[8] **giardia:** a protozoan parasite that lives inside the intestines of infected humans and
animals. It is contracted through consuming contaminated food or liquids.

---

6. ◀ **REREAD AND DISCUSS** Reread lines 115–135. With a small group,
discuss Roach's tone in these lines. Why does she refer to herself as "myself"
in lines 129–135?

7. **READ** ▶ As you read lines 136–169, continue to cite text evidence.

• In the margin, explain Roach's reaction to chicha in lines 141–149.

• Underline text describing the Achuar's reaction to the energy bar.

CLOSE READ
Notes

"I come from a tribe that eats Vienna sausages. I should be able to cope."

amoebas in the unfiltered river water it's made with. It is at this moment that Isaac's mother gets up to retrieve the chicha bowl from Patton, fill it to near overflow and present it to me.

The first thing that hits you is the smell. Fruity and fetid, a whiff of drinker's breath on a late-night bus. I put my lips to the rim of the bowl, bumpy-slimy with manioc pulp. I hold my breath and drink.

The taste is not awful. It's chalky, rummy, indifferent. But this was never about taste. It's about distaste. Did you ever drop something into a toilet and have to roll up your sleeve and retrieve it? That's how I'm feeling right now. Only I've got to keep going. I've got to lift the lid, step right in, and hunker down in the toilet bowl. As soon as the level of chicha lowers visibly, Isaac's mother will step up to refill the bowl.

I disappoint and surprise myself. I come from a tribe that eats Vienna sausages. I should be able to cope. But I can't. I cannot drink this bowl of chicha.

An idea alights. I ask Patton to hold my bowl and rummage in my backpack for the crinkle of airtight cellophane: a raspberry-chocolate Trader Joe's energy bar. The room falls abruptly quiet. Foreigner's backpacks are known to hold all manner of otherworldly wonders: sugar packets, earplugs, contact lenses.

The energy bar makes the rounds. A few of the men sniff at it. Only Isaac takes a bite. He chews vigorously at first, then stops, suddenly and with alarm, as though someone had snuck up behind him and put a gun to his head. His eyebrows bunch together like drawn drapes. His lips go all abstract and jumpy. He stands, grabs hold of a roof post, and spits forcefully. He coughs, arrghs, hawks, spits again.

© Houghton Mifflin Harcourt Publishing Company

Every few seconds, he looks back at me, his face changing channels from disgust to bewilderment and back. After a good minute of this, he hands back the energy bar, grinning now that the taste is gone, shaking his head at the foreigner's unfathomable tastes.

The way I see it, permission has been granted to back out of the next bowl of chicha.

8. **◀ REREAD**   Reread lines 153–169 to cite evidence. Why does Roach give the men the energy bar?

_____

_____

_____

SHORT RESPONSE

Cite Text Evidence   What is Roach's purpose in writing this article? How does her tone convey this purpose? Review your reading notes, and be sure to **cite text evidence** in your response.

_____

_____

_____

_____

_____

_____

_____

_____

_____

_____

© Houghton Mifflin Harcourt Publishing Company

Background Edith Wharton *(1862–1937) was born into a wealthy family in New York City. From her earliest days, Wharton displayed an exceptional visual memory. Before she was eight, she was composing stories in her head, later committing them to paper. By the time she was thirteen, she was writing sonnets. The novel that brought Wharton her first great success was* The House of Mirth *(1905), the story of a young woman crushed by the ranks of old New York when she tries to live by her own moral standards. The most celebrated American female writer of her time, she had a skeptical view of personal fulfillment. "If only we'd stop trying to be happy," she once said, "we could have a pretty good time."*

A Journey

Short Story by Edith Wharton

CLOSE READ
Notes

1. **READD** ▶ As you read lines 1–23, begin to collect and cite text evidence.

   - Underline the images that the wife sees from her berth in lines 1–6, and in the margin, note what mood they suggest.
   - Circle text describing changes in the husband in lines 7–23.
   - In the margin of the next page, explain the simile Wharton uses in lines 11–15.

As she lay in her berth, staring at the shadows overhead, the rush of the wheels was in her brain, driving her deeper and deeper into circles of wakeful lucidity. The sleeping-car had sunk into its night-silence. Through the wet window-pane she watched the sudden lights, the long stretches of hurrying blackness. Now and then she turned her head and looked through the opening in the hangings at her husband's curtains across the aisle. . . .

She wondered restlessly if he wanted anything and if she could hear him if he called. His voice had grown very weak within the last months and it irritated him when she did not hear. This irritability, this increasing childish **petulance** seemed to give expression to their imperceptible estrangement.

10

petulance:

© Houghton Mifflin Harcourt Publishing Company • Image Credits: ©Beatmann/Corbis; ©urban cam/Shutterstock

Like two faces looking at one another through a sheet of glass they were close together, almost touching, but they could not hear or feel each other: the conductivity between them was broken. She, at least, had this sense of separation, and she fancied sometimes that she saw it reflected in the look with which he supplemented his failing words. Doubtless the fault was hers. She was too impenetrably healthy to be touched by the irrelevancies of disease. Her self-reproachful tenderness was tinged with the sense of his irrationality: she had a vague feeling that there was a purpose in his helpless tyrannies. The suddenness of the change had found her so unprepared. A year ago their pulses had beat to one robust measure; both had the same **prodigal** confidence in an exhaustless future. Now their energies no longer kept step: hers still bounded ahead of life, preempting unclaimed regions of hope and activity, while his lagged behind, vainly struggling to overtake her.

prodigal:

20

    When they married, she had such arrears of living to make up: her days had been as bare as the whitewashed school-room where she forced innutritious facts upon reluctant children. His coming had broken in on the slumber of circumstance, widening the present till it became the encloser of remotest chances. But imperceptibly the horizon narrowed. Life had a grudge against her: she was never to be allowed to spread her wings.

30

    At first the doctors had said that six weeks of mild air would set him right; but when he came back this assurance was explained as having of course included a winter in a dry climate. They gave up their pretty house, storing the

2. **◀ REREAD** Reread lines 7–23. What do the contrasting descriptions of health and sickness suggest about the wife's relationship with her husband? How does she describe her own reactions to her husband's health? Support your answer with explicit textual evidence.

_____

_____

_____

_____

_____

_____

3. **READ ▶** As you read lines 24–63, continue to cite textual evidence.

- Underline text that shows the wife's negative feelings in lines 24–45.
- In the margin, describe in your own words how the husband used to be (lines 30–45).
- Underline text that describes the wife's fear in lines 46–63.

> "It frightened her to feel that this was the man she loved . . ."

wedding presents and new furniture, and went to Colorado. She had hated it there from the first. Nobody knew her or cared about her; there was no one to wonder at the good match she had made, or to envy her the new dresses and the visiting-cards which were still a surprise to her. And he kept growing worse. She felt herself beset with difficulties too evasive to be fought by so direct a temperament. She still loved him, of course; but he was gradually, undefinably ceasing to be himself. The man she had married had been strong, active, gently masterful: the male whose pleasure it is to clear a way through the material obstructions of life; but now it was she who was the protector, he who must be shielded from importunities and given his drops or his beef-juice though the skies were falling. The routine of the sick-room bewildered her; this punctual administering of medicine seemed as idle as some uncomprehended religious mummery.[1]

There were moments, indeed, when warm gushes of pity swept away her instinctive resentment of his condition, when she still found his old self in his eyes as they groped for each other through the dense medium of his weakness. But these moments had grown rare. Sometimes he frightened her: his sunken expressionless face seemed that of a stranger; his voice was weak and hoarse; his thin-lipped smile a mere muscular contraction. Her hand avoided his damp soft skin, which had lost the familiar roughness of health: she caught herself **furtively** watching him as she might have watched a strange animal. It frightened her to feel that this was the man she loved; there were hours when to tell him what she suffered seemed the one escape from her fears. But in general she judged herself more leniently, reflecting that she had perhaps been too long alone with him, and that she would feel differently when they were at home again, surrounded by her robust and buoyant family. How she had rejoiced when the doctors at last gave their consent to his going home! She knew, of course, what the decision meant; they both knew. It meant that he was to die; but they dressed the truth in hopeful euphuisms, and at times, in the joy of preparation, she really forgot the purpose of their journey, and slipped into an eager allusion to next year's plans.

furtively:

---
[1] **mummery:** a ridiculous performance or ceremony.

At last the day of leaving came. She had a dreadful fear that they would never get away; that somehow at the last moment he would fail her; that the doctors held one of their accustomed treacheries in reserve; but nothing happened. They drove to the station, he was installed in a seat with a rug over his knees and a cushion at his back, and she hung out of the window waving unregretful farewells to the acquaintances she had really never liked till then.

70   The first twenty-four hours had passed off well. He revived a little and it amused him to look out of the window and to observe the humours of the car. The second day he began to grow weary and to chafe under the **dispassionate** stare of the freckled child with the lump of chewing-gum. She had to explain to the child's mother that her husband was too ill to be disturbed: a statement received by that lady with a resentment visibly supported by the maternal sentiment of the whole car. . . .

    That night he slept badly and the next morning his temperature frightened her: she was sure he was growing worse. The day passed slowly, punctuated by the small irritations of travel. Watching his tired face, she traced in its

80 contractions every rattle and jolt of the tram, till her own body vibrated with sympathetic fatigue. She felt the others observing him too, and hovered restlessly between him and the line of interrogative eyes. The freckled child hung about him like a fly; offers of candy and picture-books failed to dislodge her: she twisted one leg around the other and watched him **imperturbably**. The porter, as he passed, lingered with vague proffers of help, probably inspired by philanthropic passengers swelling with the sense that "something ought to

dispassionate:

imperturbably:

---

4. ◀ **REREAD**   Reread lines 46–63. From what point of view is the story being told? How do you know?

_____

_____

_____

_____

---

5. **READ** ▶   As you read lines 64–105, continue to cite textual evidence.

- Underline phrases that help set the tone of the story.
- In the margin, explain why the return home is an example of situational irony (lines 95–105).

> "She had a dreadful fear . . . that the doctors held one of their accustomed treacheries in reserve . . ."

be done;" and one nervous man in a skull-cap was audibly concerned as to the possible effect on his wife's health.

The hours dragged on in a dreary inoccupation. Towards dusk she sat
90 down beside him and he laid his hand on hers. The touch startled her. He seemed to be calling her from far off. She looked at him helplessly and his smile went through her like a physical pang.

"Are you very tired?" she asked.

"No, not very."

"We'll be there soon now."

"Yes, very soon."

"This time to-morrow—"

He nodded and they sat silent. When she had put him to bed and crawled into her own berth she tried to cheer herself with the thought that in less than
100 twenty-four hours they would be in New York. Her people would all be at the station to meet her—she pictured their round unanxious faces pressing through the crowd. She only hoped they would not tell him too loudly that he was looking splendidly and would be all right in no time: the subtler sympathies developed by long contact with suffering were making her aware of a certain coarseness of texture in the family **sensibilities**.

Suddenly she thought she heard him call. She parted the curtains and listened. No, it was only a man snoring at the other end of the car. His snores had a greasy sound, as though they passed through tallow. She lay down and tried to sleep . . . Had she not heard him move? She started up trembling . . .

sensibility:

---

6. ◀ **REREAD AND DISCUSS** Reread lines 64–105. With a small group, discuss the wife's concern about the journey. Why is she worried about "her people"?

7. **READ** ▷ As you read lines 106–150, continue to cite textual evidence.

   • Underline actions the wife takes in lines 106–121.

   • In the margin, explain what is ironic, or surprising, about her actions (lines 114–121).

   • Circle text that describes a change in the wife's outlook in lines 122–132.

© Houghton Mifflin Harcourt Publishing Company

110 The silence frightened her more than any sound. He might not be able to make her hear—he might be calling her now . . . What made her think of such things? It was merely the familiar tendency of an over-tired mind to fasten itself on the most intolerable chance within the range of its forebodings. . . . Putting her head out, she listened; but she could not distinguish his breathing from that of the other pairs of lungs about her. She longed to get up and look at him, but she knew the impulse was a mere vent for her restlessness, and the fear of disturbing him restrained her. . . . The regular movement of his curtain reassured her, she knew not why; she remembered that he had wished her a cheerful good-night; and the sheer inability to endure her fears a moment

120 longer made her put them from her with an effort of her whole sound tired body. She turned on her side and slept.

She sat up stiffly, staring out at the dawn. The train was rushing through a region of bare hillocks huddled against a lifeless sky. It looked like the first day of creation. The air of the car was close, and she pushed up her window to let in the keen wind. Then she looked at her watch: it was seven o'clock, and soon the people about her would be stirring. She slipped into her clothes, smoothed her

dishevelled: **dishevelled** hair and crept to the dressing-room. When she had washed her face and adjusted her dress she felt more hopeful. It was always a struggle for her not to be cheerful in the morning. Her cheeks burned deliciously under the

130 coarse towel and the wet hair about her temples broke into strong upward tendrils. Every inch of her was full of life and elasticity. And in ten hours they would be at home!

She stepped to her husband's berth: it was time for him to take his early glass of milk. The window-shade was down, and in the dusk of the curtained enclosure she could just see that he lay sideways, with his face away from her. She leaned over him and drew up the shade. As she did so she touched one of his hands. It felt cold. . . .

She bent closer, laying her hand on his arm and calling him by name. He did not move. She spoke again more loudly; she grasped his shoulder and

140 gently shook it. He lay motionless. She caught hold of his hand again: it slipped from her limply, like a dead thing. A dead thing? . . . Her breath caught. She must see his face. She leaned forward, and hurriedly, shrinkingly, with a sickening reluctance of the flesh, laid her hands on his shoulders and turned him over. His head fell back; his face looked small and smooth; he gazed at her with steady eyes.

150 train at the next station—

In a terrifying flash of remembrance there arose before her a scene she had once witnessed in travelling, when a husband and wife, whose child had died in the train, had been thrust out at some chance station. She saw them standing on the platform with the child's body between them; she had never forgotten the dazed look with which they followed the receding train. And this was what would happen to her. Within the next hour she might find herself on the platform of some strange station, alone with her husband's body. . . . Anything but that! It was too horrible—She quivered like a creature at bay.

As she cowered there, she felt the train moving more slowly. It was coming
160 then—they were approaching a station! She saw again the husband and wife standing on the lonely platform; and with a violent gesture she drew down the shade to hide her husband's face.

Feeling dizzy, she sank down on the edge of the berth, keeping away from his outstretched body, and pulling the curtains close, so that he and she were shut into a kind of **sepulchral** twilight. She tried to think. At all costs she must conceal the fact that he was dead. But how? Her mind refused to act: she could not plan, combine. She could think of no way but to sit there, clutching the curtains, all day long. . . .

She heard the porter making up her bed; people were beginning to move
170 about the car; the dressing-room door was being opened and shut. She tried to rouse herself. At length with a supreme effort she rose to her feet, stepping into

sepulchral:

8. **◀ REREAD** Reread lines 138–150. Why is the wife's reaction to her husband's death ironic?

_____

_____

_____

_____

9. **READ ▶** As you read lines 151–188, continue to cite textual evidence.

• Underline text describing what the wife remembers.

• In the margin, explain why the wife conceals her husband's death (lines 151–162).

97

the aisle of the car and drawing the curtains tight behind her. She noticed that they still parted slightly with the motion of the car, and finding a pin in her dress she fastened them together. Now she was safe. She looked round and saw the porter. She fancied he was watching her.

"Ain't he awake yet?" he enquired.

"No," she faltered.

"I got his milk all ready when he wants it. You know you told me to have it for him by seven."

180   She nodded silently and crept into her seat.

At half-past eight the train reached Buffalo. By this time the other passengers were dressed and the berths had been folded back for the day. The porter, moving to and fro under his burden of sheets and pillows, glanced at her as he passed. At length he said: "Ain't he going to get up? You know we're ordered to make up the berths as early as we can."

She turned cold with fear. They were just entering the station.

"Oh, not yet," she stammered. "Not till he's had his milk. Won't you get it, please?"

"All right. Soon as we start again."

190   When the train moved on he reappeared with the milk. She took it from him and sat vaguely looking at it: her brain moved slowly from one idea to another, as though they were stepping-stones set far apart across a whirling flood. At length she became aware that the porter still hovered expectantly.

"Will I give it to him?" he suggested.

"Oh, no," she cried, rising. "He—he's asleep yet, I think—"

---

10. **◀ REREAD** Reread lines 151–188. Explain the dramatic irony implicit in the wife's attempts to hide her husband's death from the people on the train.

_____

_____

_____

_____

11. **READ ▷** As you read lines 189–210, continue to cite textual evidence.

- Circle the simile Wharton uses to describe the wife's mental state.
- In the margin, explain why she decides to drink the milk (lines 194–202).

© Houghton Mifflin Harcourt Publishing Company

She waited till the porter had passed on; then she unpinned the curtains and slipped behind them. In the semi-obscurity her husband's face stared up at her like a marble mask with agate eyes. The eyes were dreadful. She put out her hand and drew down the lids. Then she remembered the glass of milk in her

200 other hand: what was she to do with it? She thought of raising the window and throwing it out; but to do so she would have to lean across his body and bring her face close to his. She decided to drink the milk.

She returned to her seat with the empty glass and after a while the porter came back to get it.

"When'll I fold up his bed?" he asked.

"Oh, not now—not yet; he's ill—he's very ill. Can't you let him stay as he is? The doctor wants him to lie down as much as possible."

He scratched his head. "Well, if he's *really* sick—"

He took the empty glass and walked away, explaining to the passengers

210 that the party behind the curtains was too sick to get up just yet.

She found herself the centre of sympathetic eyes. A motherly woman with an intimate smile sat down beside her.

"I'm real sorry to hear your husband's sick. I've had a remarkable amount of sickness in my family and maybe I could assist you. Can I take a look at him?"

"Oh, no—no, please! He mustn't be disturbed."

The lady accepted the **rebuff** indulgently.

rebuff:

"Well, it's just as you say, of course, but you don't look to me as if you'd had much experience in sickness and I'd have been glad to assist you. What do you

220 generally do when your husband's taken this way?"

12. **◄ REREAD** Reread lines 203–210. Why are the porter's actions ironic? Cite evidence in your response.

_____

_____

_____

_____

13. **READ ►** As you read lines 211–239, continue to cite textual evidence.

- Underline the questions that the "motherly woman" asks.
- Circle the wife's responses.

"I—I let him sleep."

"Too much sleep ain't any too healthful either. Don't you give him any medicine?"

"Y—yes."

"Don't you wake him to take it?"

"Yes."

"When does he take the next dose?"

"Not for—two hours—"

The lady looked disappointed. "Well, if I was you I'd try giving it oftener.
230   That's what I do with my folks."

After that many faces seemed to press upon her. The passengers were on their way to the dining-car, and she was conscious that as they passed down the aisle they glanced curiously at the closed curtains. One lantern-jawed man with prominent eyes stood still and tried to shoot his projecting glance through the division between the folds. The freckled child, returning from breakfast, waylaid the passers with a buttery clutch, saying in a loud whisper, "He's sick;" and once the conductor came by, asking for tickets. She shrank into her corner and looked out of the window at the flying trees and houses, meaningless hieroglyphs of an endlessly unrolled papyrus.

240   Now and then the train stopped, and the newcomers on entering the car stared in turn at the closed curtains. More and more people seemed to pass— their faces began to blend fantastically with the images surging in her brain. . . .

Later in the day a fat man detached himself from the mist of faces. He had a creased stomach and soft pale lips. As he pressed himself into the seat facing her she noticed that he was dressed in black broadcloth, with a soiled white tie.

---

14. **◄ REREAD** Reread lines 231–239. What is the result of the conversation between the wife and the "motherly woman"? How is the wife affected? Support your answer with text evidence.

_____

_____

_____

_____

15. **READ ▶** As you read lines 240–290, continue to cite text evidence.

• Underline text used to describe the fat man in lines 243–249.

• In the margin, explain who he might be.

• Underline text describing the confusion the wife feels in lines 255–272.

100

© Houghton Mifflin Harcourt Publishing Company

"Husband's pretty bad this morning, is he?"

"Yes."

"Dear, dear! Now that's terribly distressing, ain't it?" An apostolic smile revealed his gold-filled teeth.

250 "Of course you know there's no sech thing as sickness. Ain't that a lovely thought? Death itself is but a deloosion of our grosser senses. On'y lay yourself open to the influx of the sperrit, submit yourself passively to the action of the divine force, and disease and **dissolution** will cease to exist for you. If you could indooce your husband to read this little pamphlet—"

The faces about her again grew indistinct. She had a vague recollection of hearing the motherly lady and the parent of the freckled child ardently disputing the relative advantages of trying several medicines at once, or of taking each in turn; the motherly lady maintaining that the competitive system saved time; the other objecting that you couldn't tell which remedy had effected

260 the cure; their voices went on and on, like bell-buoys droning through a fog. . . . The porter came up now and then with questions that she did not understand, but that somehow she must have answered since he went away again without repeating them; every two hours the motherly lady reminded her that her husband ought to have his drops; people left the car and others replaced them . . .

Her head was spinning and she tried to steady herself by clutching at her thoughts as they swept by, but they slipped away from her like bushes on the side of a sheer **precipice** down which she seemed to be falling. Suddenly her mind grew clear again and she found herself vividly picturing what would

270 happen when the train reached New York. She shuddered as it occurred to her that he would be quite cold and that some one might perceive he had been dead since morning.

She thought hurriedly:—"If they see I am not surprised they will suspect something. They will ask questions, and if I tell them the truth they won't believe me—no one would believe me! It will be terrible"—and she kept repeating to herself:—"I must pretend I don't know. I must pretend I don't

dissolution:

precipice:

16. **◄ REREAD** Reread lines 273–279. What new concerns occur to the narrator in these lines? How is this an example of situational irony?

_____

_____

_____

_____

know. When they open the curtains I must go up to him quite naturally—and then I must scream." . . . She had an idea that the scream would be very hard to do.

280 Gradually new thoughts crowded upon her, vivid and urgent: she tried to separate and restrain them, but they beset her clamorously, like her schoolchildren at the end of a hot day, when she was too tired to silence them. Her head grew confused, and she felt a sick fear of forgetting her part, of betraying herself by some unguarded word or look.

"I must pretend I don't know," she went on murmuring. The words had lost their significance, but she repeated them mechanically, as though they had been a magic formula, until suddenly she heard herself saying: "I can't remember, I can't remember!"

Her voice sounded very loud, and she looked about her in terror; but no 290 one seemed to notice that she had spoken.

arabesque:

As she glanced down the car her eye caught the curtains of her husband's berth, and she began to examine the monotonous **arabesques** woven through their heavy folds. The pattern was intricate and difficult to trace; she gazed fixedly at the curtains and as she did so the thick stuff grew transparent and through it she saw her husband's face—his dead face. She struggled to avert her look, but her eyes refused to move and her head seemed to be held in a vice. At last, with an effort that left her weak and shaking, she turned away; but it was of no use; close in front of her, small and smooth, was her husband's face. It seemed to be suspended in the air between her and the false braids of the 300 woman who sat in front of her. With an uncontrollable gesture she stretched out her hand to push the face away, and suddenly she felt the touch of his

repress:

smooth skin. She **repressed** a cry and half started from her seat. The woman with the false braids looked around, and feeling that she must justify her movement in some way she rose and lifted her travelling-bag from the opposite seat. She unlocked the bag and looked into it; but the first object her hand met was a small flask of her husband's, thrust there at the last moment, in the haste of departure. She locked the bag and closed her eyes . . . his face was there again, hanging between her eye-balls and lids like a waxen mask against a red curtain. . . .

310 She roused herself with a shiver. Had she fainted or slept? Hours seemed to have elapsed; but it was still broad day, and the people about her were sitting in the same attitudes as before.

---

17. (READ ▶) Read lines 291–332, and continue to cite textual evidence.

- Underline text describing the wife's confusion in lines 291–322.
- In the margin, explain what is happening in these lines.
- Underline images of death in the wife's dream (lines 323–332).

© Houghton Mifflin Harcourt Publishing Company

A sudden sense of hunger made her aware that she had eaten nothing since morning. The thought of food filled her with disgust, but she dreaded a return of faintness, and remembering that she had some biscuits in her bag she took one out and ate it. The dry crumbs choked her, and she hastily swallowed a little brandy from her husband's flask. The burning sensation in her throat acted as a counter-irritant, momentarily relieving the dull ache of her nerves. Then she felt a gently-stealing warmth, as though a soft air fanned her, and the

320   swarming fears relaxed their clutch, receding through the stillness that enclosed her, a stillness soothing as the spacious quietude of a summer day. She slept.

Through her sleep she felt the impetuous rush of the train. It seemed to be life itself that was sweeping her on with headlong **inexorable** force—sweeping her into darkness and terror, and the awe of unknown days.—Now all at once everything was still—not a sound, not a pulsation . . . She was dead in her turn, and lay beside him with smooth upstaring face. How quiet it was!—and yet she heard feet coming, the feet of the men who were to carry them away . . . She could feel too—she felt a sudden prolonged vibration, a series of hard shocks,

330   and then another plunge into darkness: the darkness of death this time—a black whirlwind on which they were both spinning like leaves, in wild uncoiling spirals, with millions and millions of the dead. . . .

She sprang up in terror. Her sleep must have lasted a long time, for the winter day had paled and the lights had been lit. The car was in confusion, and as she regained her self-possession she saw that the passengers were gathering up their wraps and bags. The woman with the false braids had brought from the dressing-room a sickly ivy-plant in a bottle, and the Christian Scientist was reversing his cuffs. The porter passed down the aisle with his impartial brush. An impersonal figure with a gold-banded cap asked for her husband's ticket. A

340   voice shouted "Baig-gage express!" and she heard the clicking of metal as the passengers handed over their checks.

inexorable:

18. **REREAD** Reread lines 323–332. Why do you think Wharton uses these deathly images in these lines?

_____

_____

19. **READ** As you read lines 333–352, continue to cite textual evidence.

• Underline text describing the porter's actions.

• In the margin, explain what happens to the wife (lines 350–352).

© Houghton Mifflin Harcourt Publishing Company

Presently her window was blocked by an expanse of sooty wall, and the train passed into the Harlem tunnel. The journey was over; in a few minutes she would see her family pushing their joyous way through the throng at the station. Her heart dilated. The worst terror was past. . . .

"We'd better get him up now, hadn't we?" asked the porter, touching her arm.

He had her husband's hat in his hand and was meditatively revolving it under his brush.

350 She looked at the hat and tried to speak; but suddenly the car grew dark. She flung up her arms, struggling to catch at something, and fell face downward, striking her head against the dead man's berth.

20. ◀ REREAD Reread lines 342–345. Explain the irony of the text "The journey was over" in line 343.

_____

_____

SHORT RESPONSE

Cite Text Evidence What do you think is the theme of "A Journey"? How does Wharton's use of irony hint at a deeper message about life that the author wants to convey? Support your response with **explicit textual evidence**.

_____

_____

_____

_____

_____

_____

_____

© Houghton Mifflin Harcourt Publishing Company

Background Pablo Neruda *(1904–1973) was a Chilean poet who won the Nobel Prize for Literature in 1971. His book* Odas Elementals (Elementary Odes) *consists of poems that delve into everyday things, often things that do not readily seem to be inspirations for poetry. Neruda has written odes to his socks, salt, and the atom, as well as the large tuna you will read about here. The odes are written for everyday people, with a form and language that are simple and clear. In a 1970 interview with* The Paris Review, *Neruda said, "I don't believe in symbols. They are simply material things. The sea, fish, birds exist for me in a material way."*

Ode to a Large Tuna in the Market

Poem by Pablo Neruda

CLOSE READ
Notes

1. **READD ▶** As you read lines 1–14, begin to collect and cite text evidence.

- Underline the first word of the poem.
- Circle figurative language that describes the tuna and the market vegetables.
- In the margin, explain the impact of the descriptions in lines 1–10.

Here,
among the market vegetables,
this torpedo
from the ocean
5 depths,
a missile
that swam,
now
lying in front of me
10 dead.

© Houghton Mifflin Harcourt Publishing Company • Image Credits: © Bettmann/Corbis; ©Sarah Snow

Surrounded
by the earth's green froth
—these lettuces,
bunches of carrots—
15 only you
lived through
the sea's truth, survived
the unknown, the
unfathomable
20 darkness, the depths
of the sea,
the great
abyss,
le grand abîme,[1]
25 only you:

varnish: **varnished**
black-pitched
witness
to that deepest night.

---

[1] **le grand abîme:** French for "the large abyss."

30 Only you:
dark bullet
barreled
from the depths,
carrying
35 only
your
one wound,
but resurgent,
always renewed,
40 locked into the current,
fins fletched[2]
like wings
in the torrent,
in the coursing
45 of
the
underwater
dark,
like a grieving arrow,
50 sea-javelin, a nerveless
oiled harpoon.

---

[2] **fletched:** feathered.

2. **◄ REREAD** Reread lines 1–14. Analyze the contrast Neruda makes between the fish and the vegetables. Cite text evidence in your answer.

_____

_____

_____

_____

_____

3. **READ ▶** As you read lines 15–51, continue to cite text evidence.

• Underline repeated phrases.

• In the margin, explain what makes the tuna unique.

© Houghton Mifflin Harcourt Publishing Company

Dead
in front of me,
catafalqued[3] king
55 of my own ocean;
once
sappy as a sprung fir
in the green turmoil,
once seed
60 to sea-quake,
tidal wave, now
simply
dead remains;
in the whole market
65 yours
was the only shape left
with purpose or direction
in this
jumbled ruin
70 of nature;

you are
a solitary man of war
among these frail vegetables,
your flanks and prow
75 black
and slippery
as if you were still
a well-oiled ship of the wind,
the only
80 true
machine
of the sea: unflawed,
undefiled,
navigating now
85 the waters of death.

_____
[3] **catafalque:** a platform used to
support a coffin.

---

4. **◀ REREAD** Reread lines 15–51. How does Neruda continue to compare
the tuna to a missile? Cite text evidence in your answer.

_____

_____

_____

_____

---

5. **READ ▶** As you read lines 52–85, continue to cite text evidence.

• Circle text that describes the ocean.

• Underline text that describes the tuna.

• In the margin, write three adjectives describing Neruda's ocean.

© Houghton Mifflin Harcourt Publishing Company

6. **◄ REREAD** What are "the waters of death" that Neruda mentions in the last line of the poem? In what way is this description ironic? Cite text evidence in your explanation.

_____

_____

_____

_____

SHORT RESPONSE

Cite Text Evidence   In the Background section, you read that Neruda does not "believe in symbols." What do you think the tuna means to him? Review your reading notes, and remember to **cite text evidence** in your response.

_____

_____

_____

_____

_____

_____

_____

_____

_____

_____

_____

_____

_____

© Houghton Mifflin Harcourt Publishing Company

The Modern World

© Houghton Mifflin Harcourt Publishing Company • Image Credits: ©Bek Shakirov/Images.com/Corbis

"Everybody gets so much information all
day long that they lose their common sense."

—Gertrude Stein

© Houghton Mifflin Harcourt Publishing Company • Image Credits: ©Eric Shadney/Images.com/Corbis

Background Tim O'Brien's *military experience in Vietnam provides much of the material for his fiction and personal narratives. In 1990, O'Brien published* The Things They Carried, *a remarkable fictional memoir about the Vietnam War and its human effects. The book is made up of interconnected stories narrated by a character named Tim O'Brien, who, the author says, is not himself.* "Ambush" *comes from that collection.*

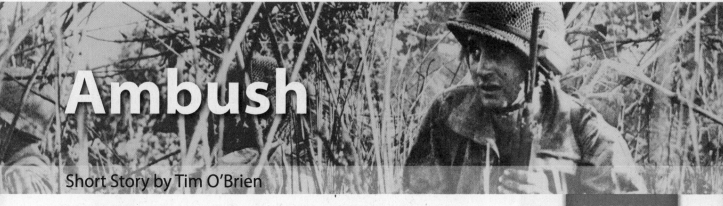

Ambush

Short Story by Tim O'Brien

CLOSE READ
Notes

1. **READ** ▶ As you read lines 1–13, begin to collect and cite text evidence.

• Underline text that explains why the narrator is telling this story.
• Circle text that explains why the narrator continues to write war stories.

When she was nine, my daughter Kathleen asked if I had ever killed anyone. She knew about the war; she knew I'd been a soldier. "You keep writing these war stories," she said, "so I guess you must've killed somebody." It was a difficult moment, but I did what seemed right, which was to say, "Of course not," and then to take her onto my lap and hold her for a while. Someday, I hope, she'll ask again. But here I want to pretend she's a grown-up. I want to tell her exactly what happened, or what I remember happening, and then I want to say to her that as a little girl she was absolutely right. This is why I keep writing war stories:

10   He was a short, slender young man of about twenty. I was afraid of him— afraid of something—and as he passed me on the trail I threw a grenade that exploded at his feet and killed him.

Or to go back:

2. ◀ **REREAD** As you reread lines 1–9, make notes in the margin about Kathleen's question, the narrator's answer at the time, and the narrator's desire to explain more.

111

Shortly after midnight we moved into the ambush site outside My Khe.
The whole platoon was there, spread out in the dense brush along the trail, and
for five hours nothing at all happened. We were working in two-man teams—
one man on guard while the other slept, switching off every two hours—and
I remember it was still dark when Kiowa shook me awake for the final watch.
The night was foggy and hot. For the first few moments I felt lost, not sure

20 about directions, groping for my helmet and weapon. I reached out and found
three grenades and lined them up in front of me; the pins had already been
straightened for quick throwing. And then for maybe half an hour I kneeled
there and waited. Very gradually, in tiny slivers, dawn began to break through
the fog, and, from my position in the brush I could see ten or fifteen meters up
the trail. The mosquitoes were fierce. I remember slapping at them, wondering
if I should wake up Kiowa and ask for some repellent, then thinking it was a
bad idea, then looking up and seeing the young man come out of the fog. He
wore black clothing and rubber sandals and a gray ammunition belt. His
shoulders were slightly stooped, his head **cocked** to the side as if listening for

30 something. He seemed at ease. He carried his weapon in one hand, muzzle
down, moving without any hurry up the center of the trail. There was no sound
at all—none that I can remember. In a way, it seemed, he was part of the
morning fog, or my own imagination, but there was also the reality of what was
happening in my stomach. I had already pulled the pin on a grenade. I had
come up to a crouch. It was entirely automatic. I did not hate the young man; I
did not see him as the enemy; I did not ponder issues of morality or politics or
military duty. I crouched and kept my head low. I tried to swallow whatever
was rising from my stomach, which tasted like lemonade, something fruity and
sour. I was terrified. There were no thoughts about killing. The grenade was to

40 make him go away—just evaporate—and I leaned back and felt my head go
empty and then felt it fill up again. I had already thrown the grenade before
telling myself to throw it. The brush was thick and I had to lob it high, not
aiming, and I remember the grenade seeming to freeze above me for an instant,

cocked:

---

3. **READ** ▶ As you read lines 14–71, continue to cite text evidence.

- Underline text describing the narrator's feelings.
- Circle text where the narrator says "I remember" in his story.
- In the margin, make an inference about how the narrator feels after he throws the grenade (lines 39-55).

> "For me, it was not a matter of live or die. I was in no real peril."

as if a camera had clicked, and I remember ducking down and holding my breath and seeing little wisps of fog rise from the earth. The grenade bounced once and rolled across the trail. I did not hear, it but there must have been a sound, because the young man dropped his weapon and began to run, just two or three quick steps, then he hesitated, swiveling to his right, and he glanced down at the grenade and tried to cover his head but never did. It occurred to

50 me then that he was about to die. I wanted to warn him. The grenade made a popping noise—not soft but not loud either—not what I'd expected—and there was a puff of dust and smoke—a small white puff—and the young man seemed to jerk upward as if pulled by invisible wires. He fell on his back. His rubber sandals had been blown off. He lay at the center of the trail, his right leg beneath him, his one eye shut, his other eye a huge star-shaped hole.

For me, it was not a matter of live or die. I was in no real **peril**. Almost certainly the young man would have passed me by. And it will always be that way.

peril:

Later, I remember Kiowa tried to tell me that the man would've died

60 anyway. He told me that it was a good kill, that I was a soldier and this was a war, that I should shape up and stop staring and ask myself what the dead man would've done if things were reversed.

None of it mattered. The words seemed far too complicated. All I could do was **gape** at the fact of the young man's body.

gape:

© Houghton Mifflin Harcourt Publishing Company • Image Credits: ©Everett Collection Inc./Alamy

Even now I haven't finished sorting it out. Sometimes I forgive myself, other times I don't. In the ordinary hours of life I try not to dwell on it, but now and then, when I'm reading a newspaper or just sitting alone in a room, I'll look up and see the young man step out of the morning fog. I'll watch him walk toward me, his shoulders slightly stooped, his head cocked to the side, 70 and he'll pass within a few yards of me and suddenly smile at some secret thought and then continue up the trail to where it bends back into the fog.

4. **◀ REREAD** Reread lines 65–71. How does the vision the narrator imagines in these lines help resolve his conflict?

_____

_____

_____

_____

SHORT RESPONSE

Cite Text Evidence What is the narrator's motivation for telling this story? Take into consideration that he doesn't tell his daughter the truth. What conclusions can you draw about the narrator? Review your reading notes, and be sure to **cite text evidence** in your response.

_____

_____

_____

_____

_____

_____

_____

_____

_____

Background *In the early 1920s, African American artists, writers, musicians, and performers were part of a great cultural movement known as the Harlem Renaissance. The huge migration to the north after World War I brought African Americans of all ages and walks of life to the thriving New York City neighborhood called Harlem. Black men and women drew on their own cultural resources—their folk traditions as well as a new urban awareness—to produce unique forms of expression. These young black writers were the founders of a new era in literature. Looking inward, they expressed what it meant to be black in a white-dominated world.*

Selections from

The Harlem Renaissance

How It Feels to Be Colored Me . . . . . . Essay by Zora Neale Hurston

The Weary Blues . . . . Poem by Langston Hughes

Zora Neale Hurston *(1891–1960) grew up in the all-black town of Eatonville, Florida. Hurston was 13 when her family fell apart: her mother died, her father remarried, and by the age of 14, Hurston was on her own. In 1925, she moved to New York to study anthropology. Encouraged by her professors, she returned to the South to collect African American folklore, which she published in the collection* Mules and Men. *Sadly, her work fell out of favor in the 1940s, and Hurston died poor and nearly forgotten.*

Langston Hughes *(1902–1967) was one of the leading poets of the Harlem Renaissance. On a March night in 1922, Hughes sat in a small Harlem cabaret and wrote "The Weary Blues." In this poem, he incorporated the many elements of his life—the music of Southern black speech, the lyrics of the first blues he heard, and traditional poetic forms he learned in school. While the body of the poem took shape quickly, it took Hughes two years to get the ending right.*

© Houghton Mifflin Harcourt Publishing Company • Image Credits: ©Bettmann/Corbis; ©Corbis; Photo by Robert W. Kelley/Time & Life Pictures/Getty Images

1. **READ ▶** As you read lines 1–25, begin to collect and cite text evidence.

   - Underline text that is comic or ironic.
   - Circle the extended metaphor in lines 14–17.
   - In the margin, explain her description of the Northerners in lines 4–13.

How It Feels to Be Colored Me
Essay by Zora Neale Hurston

extenuating:

I am colored but I offer nothing in the way of **extenuating** circumstances except the fact that I am the only Negro in the United States whose grandfather on the mother's side was *not* an Indian chief.

I remember the very day that I became colored. Up to my thirteenth year I lived in the little Negro town of Eatonville, Florida. It is exclusively a colored town. The only white people I knew passed through the town going to or coming from Orlando. The native whites rode dusty horses, the Northern tourists chugged down the sandy village road in automobiles. The town knew the Southerners and never stopped cane chewing when they passed. But the Northerners were something else again. They were peered at cautiously from behind curtains by the timid. The more venturesome would come out on the porch to watch them go past and got just as much pleasure out of the tourists as the tourists got out of the village.

The front porch might seem a daring place for the rest of the town, but it was a gallery seat to me. My favorite place was atop the gate-post. Proscenium box for a born first-nighter.[1] Not only did I enjoy the show, but I didn't mind the actors knowing that I liked it. I actually spoke to them in passing. I'd wave at them and when they returned my salute, I would say something like this: "Howdy-do-well-I-thank-you-where-you-goin'?" Usually automobile or the horse paused at this, and after a queer exchange of compliments, I would probably "go a piece of the way" with them, as we say in farthest Florida. If one of my family happened to come to the front in time to see me, of course negotiations would be rudely broken off. But even so, it is clear that I was the first "welcome-to-our-state" Floridian, and I hope the Miami Chamber of Commerce will please take notice.

---

[1] **proscenium . . . first-nighter:** A proscenium box is a box near the stage. A first-nighter is a person who attends the opening night of a performance.

During this period, white people differed from colored to me only in that they rode through town and never lived there. They liked to hear me "speak pieces" and sing and wanted to see me dance the parse-me-la,[2] and gave me generously of their small silver for doing these things, which seemed strange to me for I wanted to do them so much that I needed bribing to stop. Only they didn't know it. The colored people gave no dimes. They **deplored** any joyful tendencies in me, but I was their Zora nevertheless. I belonged to them, to the nearby hotels, to the county—everybody's Zora.

But changes came in the family when I was thirteen, and I was sent to school in Jacksonville. I left Eatonville, the town of the oleanders,[3] as Zora. When I disembarked from the riverboat at Jacksonville, she was no more. It seemed that I had suffered a sea change.[4] I was not Zora of Orange County any more, I was now a little colored girl. I found it out in certain ways. In my heart as well as in the mirror, I became a fast brown—warranted not to rub nor run.

But I am not tragically colored. There is no great sorrow dammed up in my soul, nor lurking behind my eyes. I do not mind at all. I do not belong to the sobbing school of Negrohood who hold that nature somehow has given them a low-down dirty deal and whose feelings are all hurt about it. Even in the helter-skelter skirmish that is my life, I have seen that the world is to the strong regardless of a little pigmentation more or less. No, I do not weep at the world—I am too busy sharpening my oyster knife.[5]

deplore:

---

[2] **parse-me-la:** a dance movement popular with Southern African Americans of the period.

[3] **oleanders:** evergreen shrubs with fragrant flowers.

[4] **sea change:** a complete transformation.

[5] **oyster knife:** a reference to the saying "The world is my oyster," implying that the world contains treasure waiting to be taken, like the pearl in an oyster.

---

2. **◀ REREAD** Reread lines 4–25. Explain the extended metaphor. What can you infer about Hurston's character in these lines?

_____

_____

_____

_____

3. **READ ▶** As you read lines 26–46, continue to cite text evidence.

- Underline text describing the differences between whites and blacks.

- In the margin, summarize how Zora becomes "a little colored girl."

Someone is always at my elbow reminding me that I am the grand-
daughter of slaves. It fails to register depression with me. Slavery is sixty years
in the past. The operation was successful and the patient is doing well, thank
50   you. The terrible struggle that made me an American out of a potential slave
said "On the line!" The Reconstruction said "Get set!"; and the generation
before said "Go!" I am off to a flying start and I must not halt in the stretch to
look behind and weep. Slavery is the price I paid for civilization, and the choice
was not with me. It is a bully adventure and worth all that I have paid through
my ancestors for it. No one on earth ever had a greater chance for glory. The
world to be won and nothing to be lost. It is thrilling to think—to know that for
any act of mine, I shall get twice as much praise or twice as much blame. It is
quite exciting to hold the center of the national stage, with the spectators not
knowing whether to laugh or to weep.

60   The position of my white neighbor is much more difficult. No brown
specter pulls up a chair beside me when I sit down to eat. No dark ghost
thrusts its leg against mine in bed. The game of keeping what one has is never
so exciting as the game of getting.

      I do not always feel colored. Even now I often achieve the unconscious
Zora of Eatonville before the Hegira.[6] I feel most colored when I am thrown
against a sharp white background.

      For instance at Barnard. "Beside the waters of the Hudson"[7] I feel my race.
Among the thousand white persons, I am a dark rock surged upon, overswept
by a creamy sea. I am surged upon and overswept, but through it all, I remain
70   myself. When covered by the waters, I am; and the ebb but reveals me again.

      Sometimes it is the other way around. A white person is set down in our
midst, but the contrast is just as sharp for me. For instance, when I sit in the
drafty basement that is The New World Cabaret with a white person, my color
comes. We enter chatting about any little nothing that we have in common and
are seated by the jazz waiters. In the abrupt way that jazz orchestras have, this

specter:

---

[6] **Hegira:** journey (from the name given to Muhammad's journey from Mecca to Medina
in 622).

[7] **Barnard . . . Hudson:** Barnard is the college in New York City from which Hurston
graduated in 1928. "Beside the water . . . " is a reference to the first line of the college song.
The college is located near the Hudson River.

---

4.   **READ** ▶ As you read lines 47–94, continue to cite text evidence.

- Underline examples of repetition in lines 47–59.
- Circle words and phrases that show the transformative power of the jazz
  music in lines 71–88.
- In the margin, summarize what Hurston says about slavery.

one plunges into a number. It loses no time in **circumlocutions**, but gets right down to business. It constricts the thorax and splits the heart with its tempo and narcotic harmonies. This orchestra grows rambunctious, rears on its hind legs and attacks the tonal veil with primitive fury, rending it, clawing it until it

80 breaks through to the jungle beyond. I follow those heathen—follow them exultingly. I dance wildly inside myself; I yell within, I whoop; I shake my assegai[8] above my head, I hurl it true to the mark *yeeeeooww!* I am in the jungle and living in the jungle way. My face is painted red and yellow, and my body is painted blue. My pulse is throbbing like a war drum. I want to slaughter something—give pain, give death to what, I do not know. But the piece ends. The men of the orchestra wipe their lips and rest their fingers. I creep back slowly to the **veneer** we call civilization with the last tone and find the white friend sitting motionless in his seat, smoking calmly.

"Good music they have here," he remarks, drumming the table with his

90 fingertips.

Music! The great blobs of purple and red emotion have not touched him. He has only heard what I felt. He is far away and I see him but dimly across the ocean and the continent that have fallen between us. He is so pale with his whiteness then and I am *so* colored.

At certain times I have no race, I am *me*. When I set my hat at a certain angle and saunter down Seventh Avenue, Harlem City, feeling as snooty as the lions in front of the Forty-Second Street Library, for instance. So far as my

---

[8] **assegai:** a type of light spear used in southern Africa.

circumlocutions:

veneer:

---

5. ◀ **REREAD**   Reread lines 71–94. How is Hurston affected by the jazz performance? What does it reveal about her?

_____

_____

_____

_____

_____

6. **READ** ▶   As you read lines 95–120, continue to cite text evidence.

• Underline text that shows Hurston's pride and positive feelings about herself.

• In the margin, summarize why people are like "bags of miscellany" (lines 108–120).

raiment:

feelings are concerned, Peggy Hopkins Joyce on the Boule Mich[9] with her gorgeous **raiment**, stately carriage, knees knocking together in a most

100   aristocratic manner, has nothing on me. The cosmic Zora emerges. I belong to no race nor time, I am the eternal feminine with its string of beads.

I have no separate feeling about being an American citizen and colored. I am merely a fragment of the Great Soul that surges within the boundaries. My country, right or wrong.

Sometimes, I feel discriminated against, but it does not make me angry. It merely astonishes me. How *can* any deny themselves the pleasure of my company! It's beyond me.

miscellany:

But in the main, I feel like a brown bag of **miscellany** propped against a wall. Against a wall in company with other bags, white, red, and yellow. Pour

110   out the contents, and there is discovered a jumble of small things priceless and worthless. A first-water[10] diamond, an empty spool, bits of broken glass, lengths of string, a key to a door long since crumbled away, a rusty knife-blade, old shoes saved for a road that never was and never will be, a nail bent under the weight of things too heavy for any nail, a dried flower or two, still a little fragrant. In your hand is the brown bag. On the ground before you is the jumble it held—so much like the jumble in the bags, could they be emptied, that all might be dumped in a single heap and the bags refilled without altering the content of any greatly. A bit of colored glass more or less would not matter. Perhaps that is how the Great Stuffer of Bags filled them in the first place—who

120   knows?

---

[9] **Peggy . . . Boule Mich:** a wealthy woman of Hurston's day, walking along the Boulevard Saint-Michel in Paris.

[10] **first-water:** of the highest quality or purity.

---

7. ◀ REREAD   Reread lines 108–120. What does Hurston's statement about "bags" say about human character?

_____

_____

_____

_____

_____

_____

8. **READ ▶** As you read "The Weary Blues," continue to cite text evidence.

   - Underline pairs of words with alliteration within a line.
   - Circle the words or phrases describing sadness or defeat.

The Weary Blues
Poem by Langston Hughes

Droning a drowsy syncopated[11] tune,
Rocking back and forth to a mellow **croon**,
    I heard a Negro play.
Down on Lenox Avenue[12] the other night
5 By the pale dull **pallor** of an old gas light
    He did a lazy sway. . . .
    He did a lazy sway. . . .
To the tune o' those Weary Blues.
With his ebony hands on each ivory key
10 He made that poor piano moan with melody.
    O Blues!
Swaying to and fro on his rickety stool
He played that sad raggy tune like a musical fool.
    Sweet Blues!
15 Coming from a black man's soul.
    O Blues!
In a deep song voice with a melancholy tone
I heard that Negro sing, that old piano moan—
    "Ain't got nobody in all this world,
20   Ain't got nobody but ma self.
    I's gwine to quit ma frownin'
    And put ma troubles on the shelf."
Thump, thump, thump, went his foot on the floor.
He played a few chords then he sang some more—
25   "I got the Weary Blues
    And I can't be satisfied.
    Got the Weary Blues
    And can't be satisfied—

croon:

pallor:

---

[11]**syncopated:** characterized by a shifting of stresses from normally strong to normally weak beats.

[12]**Lenox Avenue:** a main north-south street in Harlem.

© Houghton Mifflin Harcourt Publishing Company

30   I ain't happy no mo'
        And I wish that I had died."
        And far into the night he crooned that tune.
        The stars went out and so did the moon.
        The singer stopped playing and went to bed
        While the Weary Blues echoed through his head.
35   He slept like a rock or a man that's dead.

9. **◀ REREAD** Hughes was one of the first innovators of "jazz poetry"—
poetry with a jazz-like rhythm and feeling of improvisation. Reread the
poem and then describe the effect of its rhythm and repetitions on your
experience as a reader.

_____

_____

_____

_____

SHORT RESPONSE

Cite Text Evidence Discuss how Hurston's essay and Hughes's poem—in
their subject matter, style, form, and content—exemplify the themes of the
Harlem Renaissance. Review your reading notes, and **cite text evidence** in your
response.

_____

_____

_____

_____

_____

_____

_____

_____

_____

_____

Background Arthur Miller *(1915–2005) is considered one of the major dramatists of 20th-century American theater. His politics and private life often put him in the public eye (he was once married to Marilyn Monroe). The Crucible, one of his most celebrated plays, is about an entire town caught up in a mad witch-hunt. It's set in 1692, but Miller wrote it during the "Communist scare," when a witch-hunt of a different sort was being conducted on the floor of the U.S. Congress.*

from
The Crucible

Drama by Arthur Miller

CLOSE READ
Notes

CAST OF CHARACTERS
(IN ORDER OF APPEARANCE)

Reverend Samuel Parris

Betty Parris

Tituba

Abigail Williams

Susanna Walcott

Mrs. Ann Putnam

Thomas Putnam

Mercy Lewis

Mary Warren

John Proctor

Rebecca Nurse

Giles Corey

© Houghton Mifflin Harcourt Publishing Company • Image Credits: ©Bettmann/Corbis, ©Ken Glaser/Corbis Premium RF/Alamy

1. **READ ▷** As you read lines 1–40, begin to collect and cite text evidence.

   - Underline details that describe Reverend Samuel Parris.
   - Circle details that describe the setting.
   - In the margin, explain the purpose of the exposition. For whose benefit does Miller include this text?

ACT ONE
An Overture

(A small upper bedroom in the home of Reverend Samuel Parris, *Salem, Massachusetts, in the spring of the year 1692.*

   There is a narrow window at the left. Through its leaded panes the morning sunlight streams. A candle still burns near the bed, which is at the right. A chest, a chair, and a small table are the other furnishings. At the back a door opens on the landing of the stairway to the ground floor. The room gives off an air of clean spareness. The roof rafters are exposed, and the wood colors are raw and unmellowed.

   As the curtain rises, Reverend Parris *is discovered kneeling beside the bed,*
10 *evidently in prayer. His daughter,* Betty Parris, *aged ten, is lying on the bed, inert.)*

At the time of these events Parris was in his middle forties. In history he cut a villainous path, and there is very little good to be said for him. He believed he was being **persecuted** wherever he went, despite his best efforts to win people and God to his side. In meeting, he felt insulted if someone rose to shut the door without first asking his permission. He was a widower with no interest in children, or talent with them. He regarded them as young adults, and until this strange crisis he, like the rest of Salem, never conceived that the children were anything but thankful for being permitted to walk straight, eyes
20 slightly lowered, arms at the sides, and mouths shut until bidden to speak.

   His house stood in the "town"—but we today would hardly call it a village. The meeting house[1] was nearby, and from this point outward— toward the bay or inland—there were a few small-windowed, dark houses snuggling against the raw Massachusetts winter. Salem had been established hardly forty years before. To the European world the whole province was a

persecuted:

---
[1] **meeting house:** the most important building in the Puritan community, used both for worship and for meetings.

© Houghton Mifflin Harcourt Publishing Company

barbaric frontier inhabited by a sect of fanatics who, nevertheless, were shipping out products of slowly increasing quantity and value.

No one can really know what their lives were like. They had no novelists—and would not have permitted anyone to read a novel if one were handy. Their creed forbade anything resembling a theater or "vain enjoyment." They did not celebrate Christmas, and a holiday from work meant only that they must concentrate even more upon prayer.

Which is not to say that nothing broke into this strict and somber way of life. When a new farmhouse was built, friends assembled to "raise the roof," and there would be special foods cooked and probably some potent cider passed around. There was a good supply of ne'er-do-wells in Salem, who dallied at the shovelboard[2] in Bridget Bishop's tavern. Probably more than the creed, hard work kept the morals of the place from spoiling, for the people were forced to fight the land like heroes for every grain of corn, and no man had very much time for fooling around.

That there were some jokers, however, is indicated by the practice of appointing a two-man patrol whose duty was to "walk forth in the time of God's worship to take notice of such as either lye about the meeting house, without attending to the word and ordinances, or that lye at home or in the fields without giving good account thereof, and to take the names of such persons, and to present them to the magistrates, whereby they may be accordingly proceeded against." This **predilection** for minding other people's business was time-honored among the people of Salem, and it undoubtedly created many of the suspicions which were to feed the coming madness. It was also, in my opinion, one of the things that a John Proctor would rebel against, for the time of the armed camp had almost passed, and since the country was reasonably—although not wholly—safe, the old disciplines were beginning to rankle. But, as in all such matters, the issue

---

[2] **shovelboard:** a game in which a coin or disc is shoved across a board by hand.

---

2. ◀ REREAD Reread lines 28–40. What commonalities kept the people of the Massachusetts colony together? Cite evidence from the text.

_____

_____

_____

3. READ ▶ As you read lines 41–77, continue to cite textual evidence.

- Underline text describing things the people of Salem were suspicious of.
- Circle text describing the realities of life in a new colony.
- In the margin, describe the people of Salem in your own words (lines 56–77).

barbaric:

predilection:

© Houghton Mifflin Harcourt Publishing Company

was not clear-cut, for danger was still a possibility, and in unity still lay the best promise of safety.

The edge of the wilderness was close by. The American continent stretched endlessly west, and it was full of mystery for them. It stood, dark and threatening, over their shoulders night and day, for out of it Indian tribes marauded from time to time, and Reverend Parris had parishioners who had lost relatives to these heathen.

The parochial snobbery of these people was partly responsible for their failure to convert the Indians. Probably they also preferred to take land from heathens rather than from fellow Christians. At any rate, very few Indians were converted, and the Salem folk believed that the virgin forest was the Devil's last preserve, his home base and the citadel of his final stand. To the best of their knowledge the American forest was the last place on earth that was not paying homage to God.

For these reasons, among others, they carried about an air of innate resistance, even of persecution. Their fathers had, of course, been persecuted in England. So now they and their church found it necessary to deny any other sect its freedom, lest their New Jerusalem[3] be defiled and corrupted by wrong ways and deceitful ideas.

They believed, in short, that they held in their steady hands the candle that would light the world. We have inherited this belief, and it has helped and hurt us. It helped them with the discipline it gave them. They were a dedicated folk, by and large, and they had to be to survive the life they had chosen or been born into in this country.

The proof of their belief's value to them may be taken from the opposite character of the first Jamestown settlement, farther south, in Virginia. The Englishmen who landed there were motivated mainly by a hunt for profit. They had thought to pick off the wealth of the new country and then return

---

[3] **New Jerusalem:** in Christianity, a heavenly city and the last resting place of the souls saved by Jesus. It was considered the ideal city, and Puritans modeled their communities after it.

---

4. **◀ REREAD** Reread lines 61–77. How did the wilderness setting and proximity to the Indians affect the beliefs of "the Salem folk"?

_____

_____

_____

© Houghton Mifflin Harcourt Publishing Company

rich to England. They were a band of individualists, and a much more **ingratiating** group than the Massachusetts men. But Virginia destroyed them. Massachusetts tried to kill off the Puritans, but they combined; they set up a communal society which, in the beginning, was little more than an armed camp with an autocratic and very devoted leadership. It was, however, an autocracy by consent, for they were united from top to bottom by a commonly held ideology whose **perpetuation** was the reason and justification for all their sufferings. So their self-denial, their
90 purposefulness, their suspicion of all vain pursuits, their hard-handed justice, were altogether perfect instruments for the conquest of this space so antagonistic to man.

But the people of Salem in 1692 were not quite the dedicated folk that arrived on the *Mayflower*. A vast differentiation had taken place, and in their own time a revolution had unseated the royal government and substituted a junta which was at this moment in power.[4] The times, to their eyes, must have been out of joint, and to the common folk must have seemed as insoluble and complicated as do ours today. It is not hard to see how easily many could have been led to believe that the time of confusion
100 had been brought upon them by deep and darkling forces. No hint of such speculation appears on the court record, but social disorder in any age breeds such mystical suspicions, and when, as in Salem, wonders are brought forth from below the social surface, it is too much to expect people to hold back very long from laying on the victims with all the force of their frustrations.

ingratiating:

perpetuation:

---

[4] **a junta . . . power:** *Junta* is a Spanish term meaning "a small, elite ruling council." The reference here is to the group that led England's Glorious Revolution of 1688–1689.

---

5. **READ ▷** As you read lines 78–105, continue to cite textual evidence.

   • Underline details that describe the Massachusetts colony.
   • Circle text describing the "character" of the Jamestown settlement.
   • In the margin, explain why the Massachusetts colony survived.

6. **◁ REREAD** Reread lines 93–105. According to Miller, what effect does social disorder have on the people of Salem?

_____

_____

_____

_____

© Houghton Mifflin Harcourt Publishing Company

The Salem tragedy, which is about to begin in these pages, developed from a paradox. It is a paradox in whose grip we still live, and there is no prospect yet that we will discover its resolution. Simply, it was this: for good purposes, even high purposes, the people of Salem developed a theocracy, a

110 combine of state and religious power whose function was to keep the community together, and to prevent any kind of disunity that might open it to destruction by material or ideological enemies. It was forged for a necessary purpose and accomplished that purpose. But all organization is and must be grounded on the idea of exclusion and prohibition, just as two objects cannot occupy the same space. Evidently the time came in New England when the repressions of order were heavier than seemed warranted by the dangers against which the order was organized. The witch-hunt was

manifestation:

a perverse **manifestation** of the panic which set in among all classes when the balance began to turn toward greater individual freedom.

120 When one rises above the individual villainy displayed, one can only pity them all, just as we shall be pitied someday. It is still impossible for man to organize his social life without repressions, and the balance has yet to be struck between order and freedom.

The witch-hunt was not, however, a mere repression. It was also, and as importantly, a long overdue opportunity for everyone so inclined to express publicly his guilt and sins, under the cover of accusations against the victims. It suddenly became possible—and patriotic and holy—for a man to say that Martha Corey had come into his bedroom at night, and that, while his wife was sleeping at his side, Martha laid herself down on his chest and

130 "nearly suffocated him." Of course it was her spirit only, but his satisfaction at confessing himself was no lighter than if it had been Martha herself. One could not ordinarily speak such things in public.

---

7. **READ ▷** As you read lines 106–140, continue to cite textual evidence.

   • Underline text describing the control the Puritan leaders exerted over the community.

   • In the margin, explain the paradox of the "Salem tragedy" in your own words.

8. **◁ REREAD** Reread lines 124–140. What role did "long-held hatreds of neighbors" have in the witch-hunt? Cite evidence from the text.

_____

_____

_____

© Houghton Mifflin Harcourt Publishing Company

Long-held hatreds of neighbors could now be openly expressed, and vengeance taken, despite the Bible's charitable **injunctions**. Land-lust which had been expressed before by constant bickering over boundaries and deeds, could now be elevated to the arena of morality; one could cry witch against one's neighbor and feel perfectly justified in the bargain. Old scores could be settled on a plane of heavenly combat between Lucifer and the Lord; suspicions and the envy of the miserable toward the happy could and
140 did burst out in the general revenge.

injunctions:

(Reverend Parris *is praying now, and, though we cannot hear his words, a sense of his confusion hangs about him. He mumbles, then seems about to weep; then he weeps, then prays again; but his daughter does not stir on the bed.*

The door opens, and his Negro slave enters. Tituba *is in her forties. Parris brought her with him from Barbados, where he spent some years as a merchant before entering the ministry. She enters as one does who can no longer bear to be barred from the sight of her beloved, but she is also very frightened because her slave sense has warned her that, as always, trouble in this house eventually lands on her back.*)

150 **Tituba** (*already taking a step backward*). My Betty be hearty soon?
Parris. Out of here!
Tituba (*backing to the door*). My Betty not goin' die . . .
Parris (*scrambling to his feet in a fury*). Out of my sight! (*She is gone.*) Out of my—(*He is overcome with sobs. He clamps his teeth against them and closes the door and leans against it, exhausted.*) Oh, my God! God help me! (*Quaking with fear, mumbling to himself through his sobs, he goes to the bed and gently takes* Betty's *hand.*) Betty. Child. Dear child. Will you wake, will you open up your eyes! Betty, little one . . .

(*He is bending to kneel again when his niece,* Abigail Williams, *seventeen,*
160 *enters—a strikingly beautiful girl, an orphan, with an endless capacity for* **dissembling**. *Now she is all worry and apprehension and propriety.*)

dissembling:

Abigail. Uncle? (*He looks to her.*) Susanna Walcott's here from Doctor Griggs.
Parris. Oh? Let her come, let her come.
Abigail (*leaning out the door to call to* Susanna, *who is down the hall a few steps*). Come in, Susanna.

9. **READ ▶** As you read lines 141–180, continue to cite textual evidence.

   • Underline text that helps you understand Reverend Parris.
   • Circle details that describe Abigail.
   • In the margin, explain the initial conflict in this section.

© Houghton Mifflin Harcourt Publishing Company

(Susanna Walcott, *a little younger than* Abigail, *a nervous, hurried girl, enters.*)

Parris (*eagerly*). What does the doctor say, child?

Susanna (*craning around* Parris *to get a look at* Betty). He bid me come and tell you, reverend sir, that he cannot discover no medicine for it in his books.

170 **Parris.** Then he must search on.

Susanna. Aye, sir, he have been searchin' his books since he left you, sir. But he bid me tell you, that you might look to unnatural things for the cause of it.

Parris (*his eyes going wide*). No—no. There be no unnatural cause here. Tell him I have sent for Reverend Hale of Beverly, and Mr. Hale will surely confirm that. Let him look to medicine and put out all thought of unnatural causes here. There be none.

Susanna. Aye, sir. He bid me tell you. (*She turns to go.*)

Abigail. Speak nothin' of it in the village, Susanna.

Parris. Go directly home and speak nothing of unnatural causes.

180 **Susanna.** Aye, sir. I pray for her. (*She goes out.*)

Abigail. Uncle, the rumor of witchcraft is all about; I think you'd best go down and deny it yourself. The parlor's packed with people, sir. I'll sit with her.

Parris (*pressed, turns on her*). And what shall I say to them? That my daughter and my niece I discovered dancing like heathen in the forest?

Abigail. Uncle, we did dance; let you tell them I confessed it—and I'll be whipped if I must be. But they're speakin' of witchcraft. Betty's not witched.

Parris. Abigail, I cannot go before the congregation when I know you have not opened with me. What did you do with her in the forest?

Abigail. We did dance, uncle, and when you leaped out of the bush so

190 suddenly, Betty was frightened and then she fainted. And there's the whole of it.

Parris. Child. Sit you down.

Abigail (*quavering, as she sits*). I would never hurt Betty. I love her dearly.

---

10. ◀ **REREAD** Reread lines 166–180. Why do Parris and Abigail tell Susanna to "speak nothing of unnatural causes"? Cite examples from the text.

_____

_____

_____

11. **READ** ▶ As you read lines 181–235, continue to cite textual evidence.

- Underline Parris's references to witchcraft.
- Circle statements Abigail makes about her behavior.
- In the margin, explain Abigail's description of what happened in the forest.

© Houghton Mifflin Harcourt Publishing Company

> ... the rumor of witchcraft
> is all about; I think you'd best
> go down and deny it yourself.

Parris. Now look you, child, your punishment will come in its time. But if you trafficked with[5] spirits in the forest I must know it now, for surely my enemies will, and they will ruin me with it.

Abigail. But we never **conjured** spirits.

Parris. Then why can she not move herself since midnight? This child is desperate! (Abigail *lowers her eyes.*) It must come out—my enemies will bring it

200 out. Let me know what you done there. Abigail, do you understand that I have many enemies?

Abigail. I have heard of it, uncle.

Parris. There is a faction that is sworn to drive me from my pulpit. Do you understand that?

Abigail. I think so, sir.

Parris. Now then, in the midst of such disruption, my own household is discovered to be the very center of some obscene practice. Abominations are done in the forest—

Abigail. It were sport, uncle!

210 **Parris** (*pointing at* Betty). You call this sport? (*She lowers her eyes. He pleads.*) Abigail, if you know something that may help the doctor, for God's sake tell it to me. (*She is silent.*) I saw Tituba waving her arms over the fire when I came on you. Why was she doing that? And I heard a screeching and **gibberish** coming from her mouth. She were swaying like a dumb beast over that fire!

Abigail. She always sings her Barbados songs, and we dance.

Parris. I cannot blink what I saw, Abigail, for my enemies will not blink it. I saw a dress lying on the grass.

Abigail (*innocently*). A dress?

Parris (*It is very hard to say*). Aye, a dress. And I thought I saw—someone

220 naked running through the trees!

Abigail (*in terror*). No one was naked! You mistake yourself, uncle!

conjured:

gibberish:

---

[5] **trafficked with:** met with.

---

12. ◀ **REREAD AND DISCUSS** Reread lines 198–208. In a small group, discuss Parris's conflict. Who are his enemies and why is he afraid of them?

© Houghton Mifflin Harcourt Publishing Company

abomination:

Parris (*with anger*). I saw it! (*He moves from her. Then, resolved*) Now tell me true, Abigail. And I pray you feel the weight of truth upon you, for now my ministry's at stake, my ministry and perhaps your cousin's life. Whatever **abomination** you have done, give me all of it now, for I dare not be taken unaware when I go before them down there.

Abigail. There is nothin' more. I swear it, uncle.

Parris (*studies her, then nods, half convinced*). Abigail, I have fought here three long years to bend these stiff-necked people to me, and now, just now when

230 some good respect is rising for me in the parish, you compromise my very character. I have given you a home, child, I have put clothes upon your back— now give me upright answer. Your name in the town—it is entirely white, is it not?

Abigail (*with an edge of resentment*). Why, I am sure it is, sir. There be no blush about my name.[6]

Parris (*to the point*). Abigail, is there any other cause than you have told me, for your being discharged from Goody[7] Proctor's service? I have heard it said, and I tell you as I heard it, that she comes so rarely to the church this year for she will not sit so close to something soiled. What signified that remark?

240 **Abigail.** She hates me, uncle, she must, for I would not be her slave. It's a bitter woman, a lying, cold, sniveling woman, and I will not work for such a woman!

Parris. She may be. And yet it has troubled me that you are now seven month out of their house, and in all this time no other family has ever called for your service.

Abigail. They want slaves, not such as I. Let them send to Barbados for that. I will not black my face for any of them! (*with ill-concealed resentment at him*)

begrudge:

Do you **begrudge** my bed, uncle?

Parris. No—no.

Abigail (*in a temper*). My name is good in the village! I will not have it said my

250 name is soiled! Goody Proctor is a gossiping liar!

(*Enter Mrs. Ann Putnam. She is a twisted soul of forty-five, a death-ridden woman, haunted by dreams.*)

Parris (*as soon as the door begins to open*). No—no, I cannot have anyone. (*He sees her, and a certain deference springs into him, although his worry remains.*) Why, Goody Putnam, come in.

---

[6] **There be . . . my name:** There is nothing wrong with my reputation.
[7] **Goody:** short for *Goodwife*, the Puritan equivalent of *Mrs.*

---

13. **READD** ▶ As you read lines 236–293, continue to cite textual evidence.

- Underline statements Abigail and Parris make about Goody Proctor.
- Circle mentions of witchcraft.
- In the margin, tell how Reverend Parris's and Mrs. Putnam's opinions differ.

© Houghton Mifflin Harcourt Publishing Company

Mrs. Putnam (*full of breath, shiny-eyed*). It is a marvel. It is surely a stroke of hell upon you.

Parris. No, Goody Putnam, it is—

Mrs. Putnam (*glancing at* Betty). How high did she fly, how high?

Parris. No, no, she never flew—

Mrs. Putnam (*very pleased with it*). Why, it's sure she did. Mr. Collins saw her goin' over Ingersoll's barn, and come down light as bird, he says!

Parris. Now, look you, Goody Putnam, she never—

(*Enter* Thomas Putnam, *a well-to-do, hard-handed landowner, near fifty.*) Oh, good morning, Mr. Putnam.

Putnam. It is a **providence** the thing is out now! It is a providence. (*He goes directly to the bed.*)

Parris. What's out, sir, what's—?

(Mrs. Putnam *goes to the bed.*)

Putnam (*looking down at* Betty). Why, *her* eyes is closed! Look you, Ann.

Mrs. Putnam. Why, that's strange. (*to Parris*) Ours is open.

Parris (*shocked*). Your Ruth is sick?

Mrs. Putnam (*with vicious certainty*). I'd not call it sick; the Devil's touch is heavier than sick. It's death, y'know, it's death drivin' into them, forked and hoofed.

Parris. Oh, pray not! Why, how does Ruth ail?

Mrs. Putnam. She ails as she must—she never waked this morning, but her eyes open and she walks, and hears naught, sees naught, and cannot eat. Her soul is taken, surely.

(Parris *is struck.*)

Putnam (*as though for further details*). They say you've sent for Reverend Hale of Beverly?

Parris (*with dwindling* **conviction** *now*). A precaution only. He has much experience in all demonic arts, and I—

Mrs. Putnam. He has indeed; and found a witch in Beverly last year, and let you remember that.

Parris. Now, Goody Ann, they only thought that were a witch, and I am certain there be no element of witchcraft here.

---

14. **◀ REREAD** Reread lines 236–250. What might the Reverend Parris be insinuating here? Support your answer with explicit textual evidence.

_____

_____

_____

providence:

conviction:

© Houghton Mifflin Harcourt Publishing Company

Putnam. No witchcraft! Now look you, Mr. Parris—

290 **Parris.** Thomas, Thomas, I pray you, leap not to witchcraft. I know that you—you least of all, Thomas, would ever wish so disastrous a charge laid upon me. We cannot leap to witchcraft. They will howl me out of Salem for such corruption in my house.

A word about Thomas Putnam. He was a man with many grievances, at least one of which appears justified. Some time before, his wife's brother-in-law, James Bayley, had been turned down as minister of Salem. Bayley had all the qualifications, and a two-thirds vote into the bargain, but a faction stopped his acceptance, for reasons that are not clear.

300 Thomas Putnam was the eldest son of the richest man in the village. He had fought the Indians at Narragansett,[8] and was deeply interested in parish affairs. He undoubtedly felt it poor payment that the village should so blatantly disregard his candidate for one of its more important offices, especially since he regarded himself as the intellectual superior of most of the people around him.

vindictive:

His **vindictive** nature was demonstrated long before the witchcraft began. Another former Salem minister, George Burroughs, had had to borrow money to pay for his wife's funeral, and, since the parish was remiss in his salary, he was soon bankrupt. Thomas and his brother John had Burroughs jailed for debts the man did not owe. The incident is important

310 only in that Burroughs succeeded in becoming minister where Bayley,

motif:

Thomas Putnam's brother-in-law, had been rejected; the **motif** of resentment is clear here. Thomas Putnam felt that his own name and the honor of his family had been smirched by the village; and he meant to right matters however he could.

Another reason to believe him a deeply embittered man was his attempt to break his father's will, which left a disproportionate amount to a stepbrother. As with every other public cause in which he tried to force his way, he failed in this.

---

[8] **fought the Indians at Narragansett:** The Puritans fought a series of battles against the Narragansett Indians over territory that both groups had settled on.

---

15. **READ ▶** As you read lines 294–323, continue to cite textual evidence.

- Underline text that describes Thomas Putnam's character.
- Circle text explaining his resentment.
- In the margin, explain the conclusion Miller draws about the effects of Putnam's bitterness (lines 319–323).

© Houghton Mifflin Harcourt Publishing Company

So it is not surprising to find that so many accusations against people are in the handwriting of Thomas Putnam, or that his name is so often found as a witness corroborating the supernatural testimony, or that his daughter led the crying-out at the most opportune junctures of the trials, especially when—But we'll speak of that when we come to it.

320

Putnam (*At the moment he is intent upon getting* Parris, *for whom he has only contempt, to move toward the abyss*). Mr. Parris, I have taken your part in all **contention** here, and I would continue; but I cannot if you hold back in this. There are hurtful, vengeful spirits layin' hands on these children.

Parris. But, Thomas, you cannot—

Putnam. Ann! Tell Mr. Parris what you have done.

330

Mrs. Putnam. Reverend Parris, I have laid seven babies unbaptized in the earth. Believe me, sir, you never saw more hearty babies born. And yet, each would wither in my arms the very night of their birth. I have spoke nothin', but my heart has clamored intimations.[9] And now, this year, my Ruth, my only—I see her turning strange. A secret child she has become this year, and shrivels like a sucking mouth were pullin' on her life too. And so I thought to send her to your Tituba—

Parris. To Tituba! What may Tituba—?

Mrs. Putnam. Tituba knows how to speak to the dead, Mr. Parris.

Parris. Goody Ann, it is a formidable sin to conjure up the dead!

---

[9] **clamored intimations:** nagging suspicions.

contention:

---

16. (◀ REREAD) Reread lines 294–323. After reading this background information, what effect do you think Thomas Putnam will have in the play? Support your answer with explicit textual evidence.

_____

_____

_____

_____

17. (READ ▶) As you read lines 324–379, continue to cite textual evidence.

- Underline events that have caused Mrs. Putnam to believe something wicked is at play.

- Circle the claims the Putnams make about recent events.

- In the margin, tell how the Putnams raise the level of hysteria in the town.

© Houghton Mifflin Harcourt Publishing Company

340 **Mrs. Putnam.** I take it on my soul, but who else may surely tell us what person murdered my babies?

Parris (*horrified*). Woman!

Mrs. Putnam. They were murdered, Mr. Parris! And mark this proof! Mark it! Last night my Ruth were ever so close to their little spirits; I know it, sir. For how else is she struck dumb now except some power of darkness would stop her mouth? It is a marvelous sign, Mr. Parris!

Putnam. Don't you understand it, sir? There is a murdering witch among us, bound to keep herself in the dark. (Parris *turns to* Betty, *a frantic terror rising in him*.) Let your enemies make of it what they will, you cannot blink it more.

350 **Parris** (*to* Abigail). Then you were conjuring spirits last night.

Abigail (*whispering*). Not I, sir—Tituba and Ruth.

Parris (*turns now, with new fear, and goes to* Betty, *looks down at her, and then, gazing off*). Oh, Abigail, what proper payment for my charity! Now I am undone.

Putnam. You are not undone! Let you take hold here. Wait for no one to charge you—declare it yourself. You have discovered witchcraft—

Parris. In my house? In my house, Thomas? They will topple me with this! They will make of it a—

(*Enter* Mercy Lewis, *the* Putnams' *servant, a fat, sly, merciless girl of eighteen.*)

360 **Mercy.** Your pardons. I only thought to see how Betty is.

Putnam. Why aren't you home? Who's with Ruth?

Mercy. Her grandma come. She's improved a little, I think—she give a powerful sneeze before.

Mrs. Putnam. Ah, there's a sign of life!

Mercy. I'd fear no more, Goody Putnam. It were a grand sneeze; another like it will shake her wits together, I'm sure. (*She goes to the bed to look.*)

Parris. Will you leave me now, Thomas? I would pray a while alone.

Abigail. Uncle, you've prayed since midnight. Why do you not go down and—

Parris. No—no. (*to* Putnam) I have no answer for that crowd. I'll wait till Mr.

370 Hale arrives. (*to get* Mrs. Putnam *to leave*) If you will, Goody Ann . . .

18. ◀ REREAD AND DISCUSS In a small group, discuss the significance of Abigail's whispered line: "Not I, sir—Tituba and Ruth" (line 351).

© Houghton Mifflin Harcourt Publishing Company

Putnam. Now look you, sir. Let you strike out against the Devil, and the village will bless you for it! Come down, speak to them—pray with them. They're thirsting for your word, Mister! Surely you'll pray with them.

Parris (*swayed*). I'll lead them in a psalm, but let you say nothing of witchcraft yet. I will not discuss it. The cause is yet unknown. I have had enough contention since I came; I want no more.

Mrs. Putnam. Mercy, you go home to Ruth, d'y'hear?

Mercy. Aye, mum.

(Mrs. Putnam *goes out.*)

380 **Parris** (*to* Abigail). If she starts for the window, cry for me at once.

Abigail. I will, uncle.

Parris (*to* Putnam). There is a terrible power in her arms today. (*He goes out with* Putnam.)

Abigail (*with hushed **trepidation***). How is Ruth sick?

trepidation:

Mercy. It's weirdish, I know not—she seems to walk like a dead one since last night.

Abigail (*turns at once and goes to* Betty, *and now, with fear in her voice*). Betty? (Betty *doesn't move. She shakes her.*) Now stop this! Betty! Sit up now! (Betty *doesn't stir.* Mercy *comes over.*)

390 **Mercy.** Have you tried beatin' her? I gave Ruth a good one and it waked her for a minute. Here, let me have her.

Abigail (*holding* Mercy *back*). No, he'll be comin' up. Listen, now; if they be questioning us, tell them we danced—I told him as much already.

Mercy. Aye. And what more?

Abigail. He knows Tituba conjured Ruth's sisters to come out of the grave.

Mercy. And what more?

Abigail. He saw you naked.

Mercy (*clapping her hands together with a frightened laugh*). Oh, Jesus!

(*Enter* Mary Warren, *breathless. She is seventeen, a **subservient**, naive, lonely*

subservient:

400 *girl.*)

Mary Warren. What'll we do? The village is out! I just come from the farm; the whole country's talkin' witchcraft! They'll be callin' us witches, Abby!

Mercy (*pointing and looking at* Mary Warren). She means to tell, I know it.

Mary Warren. Abby, we've got to tell. Witchery's a hangin' error, a hangin' like they done in Boston two year ago! We must tell the truth, Abby! You'll only be whipped for dancin', and the other things!

---

19. **READ ▷** As you read lines 380–442, continue to cite textual evidence.

- Underline new details about what really happened in the woods.
- Circle text that describes the feelings of the girls.
- In the margin, explain why the girls are afraid.

© Houghton Mifflin Harcourt Publishing Company

Abigail. Oh, *we'll* be whipped!

Mary Warren. I never done none of it, Abby. I only looked!

Mercy (*moving menacingly toward* Mary). Oh, you're a great one for lookin',
410 aren't you, Mary Warren? What a grand peeping courage you have!
(Betty, *on the bed, whimpers.* Abigail *turns to her at once.*)

Abigail. Betty? (*She goes to* Betty.) Now, Betty, dear, wake up now. It's Abigail.
(*She sits* Betty *up and furiously shakes her.*) I'll beat you, Betty! (Betty
whimpers.) My, you seem improving. I talked to your papa and I told him
everything. So there's nothing to—

Betty (*darts off the bed, frightened of* Abigail, *and flattens herself against the
wall*). I want my mama!

Abigail (*with alarm, as she cautiously approaches* Betty). What ails you, Betty?
Your mama's dead and buried.

420 **Betty.** I'll fly to Mama. Let me fly! (*She raises her arms as though to fly, and
streaks for the window, gets one leg out.*)

Abigail (*pulling her away from the window*). I told him everything; he knows
now, he knows everything we—

Betty. You drank blood, Abby! You didn't tell him that!

Abigail. Betty, you never say that again! You will never—

Betty. You did, you did! You drank a charm to kill John Proctor's wife! You
drank a charm to kill Goody Proctor!

Abigail (*smashes her across the face*). Shut it! Now shut it!

dissolves:

Betty (*collapsing on the bed*). Mama, Mama! (*She* **dissolves** *into sobs.*)

430 **Abigail.** Now look you. All of you. We danced. And Tituba conjured Ruth
Putnam's dead sisters. And that is all. And mark this. Let either of you breathe
a word, or the edge of a word, about the other things, and I will come to you in
the black of some terrible night and I will bring a pointy reckoning that will
shudder you.[10] And you know I can do it; I saw Indians smash my dear parents'
heads on the pillow next to mine, and I have seen some reddish work done at
night, and I can make you wish you had never seen the sun go down! (*She goes
to* Betty *and roughly sits her up.*) Now, you—sit up and stop this!

inert:

(*But* Betty *collapses in her hands and lies* **inert** *on the bed.*)

Mary Warren (*with hysterical fright*). What's got her? (Abigail *stares in fright*
440 *at* Betty.) Abby, she's going to die! It's a sin to conjure, and we—

Abigail (*starting for* Mary). I say shut it, Mary Warren!

(*Enter* John Proctor. *On seeing him,* Mary Warren *leaps in fright.*)

---

[10] **bring . . . shudder you:** inflict a terrifying punishment on you.

20. ◀ REREAD AND DISCUSS   Reread lines 428–437. In a small group, discuss
what you find out about Abigail. In what way does she affect the other girls?

© Houghton Mifflin Harcourt Publishing Company

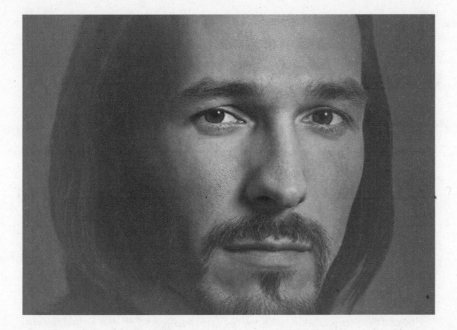

Proctor was a farmer in his middle thirties. He need not have been a
partisan of any faction in the town, but there is evidence to suggest that he
had a sharp and biting way with hypocrites. He was the kind of man—
powerful of body, even-tempered, and not easily led—who cannot refuse
support to partisans without drawing their deepest resentment. In Proctor's
presence a fool felt his foolishness instantly—and a Proctor is always
marked for calumny[11] therefore.

450   But as we shall see, the steady manner he displays does not spring from
an untroubled soul. He is a sinner, a sinner not only against the moral
fashion of the time, but against his own vision of decent conduct. These
people had no ritual for the washing away of sins. It is another trait we
inherited from them, and it has helped to discipline us as well as to breed
hypocrisy among us. Proctor, respected and even feared in Salem, has come
to regard himself as a kind of fraud. But no hint of this has yet appeared on
the surface, and as he enters from the crowded parlor below it is a man in
his prime we see, with a quiet confidence and an unexpressed, hidden force.
Mary Warren, his servant, can barely speak for embarrassment and fear.

partisan:

hypocrisy:

[11] **marked for calumny:** singled out to have lies told about him.

21. **READ ▶** As you read lines 443–459, continue to cite textual evidence.
- Underline details that describe John Proctor's best qualities.
- Circle details that show Proctor's worst qualities.

22. **◀ REREAD AND DISCUSS** Reread lines 443–459. In a small group, discuss
John Proctor's inner struggle.

139

460 **Mary Warren.** Oh! I'm just going home, Mr. Proctor.

Proctor. Be you foolish, Mary Warren? Be you deaf? I forbid you leave the house, did I not? Why shall I pay you? I am looking for you more often than my cows!

Mary Warren. I only come to see the great doings in the world.

Proctor. I'll show you a great doin' on your arse one of these days. Now get you home; my wife is waitin' with your work! (*Trying to retain a shred of dignity, she goes slowly out.*)

titillated:

Mercy Lewis (*both afraid of him and strangely **titillated***). I'd best be off. I have my Ruth to watch. Good morning, Mr. Proctor.

470 (Mercy *sidles out. Since* Proctor's *entrance,* Abigail *has stood as though on tiptoe, absorbing his presence, wide-eyed. He glances at her, then goes to* Betty *on the bed.*)

Abigail. Gah! I'd almost forgot how strong you are, John Proctor!

Proctor (*looking at* Abigail *now, the faintest suggestion of a knowing smile on his face*). What's this mischief here?

Abigail (*with a nervous laugh*). Oh, she's only gone silly somehow.

Proctor. The road past my house is a pilgrimage to Salem all morning. The town's mumbling witchcraft.

winningly:

Abigail. Oh, posh! (***Winningly** she comes a little closer, with a confidential,*

480 *wicked air.*) We were dancin' in the woods last night, and my uncle leaped in on us. She took fright, is all.

Proctor (*his smile widening*). Ah, you're wicked yet, aren't y'! (*A trill of expectant laughter escapes her, and she dares come closer, feverishly looking into his eyes.*) You'll be clapped in the stocks before you're twenty.

(*He takes a step to go, and she springs into his path.*)

Abigail. Give me a word, John. A soft word. (*Her concentrated desire destroys his smile.*)

Proctor. No, no, Abby. That's done with.

Abigail (*tauntingly*). You come five mile to see a silly girl fly? I know you

490 better.

Proctor (*setting her firmly out of his path*). I come to see what mischief your uncle's brewin' now. (*with final emphasis*) Put it out of mind, Abby.

---

23. **READ ▶** As you read lines 460–523, continue to cite textual evidence.

• Underline details that show Abigail's true feelings for John Proctor.

• In the margin, make an inference about what happened between them.

© Houghton Mifflin Harcourt Publishing Company

Abigail (*grasping his hand before he can release her*). John—I am waitin' for you every night.

Proctor. Abby, I never give you hope to wait for me.

Abigail (*now beginning to anger—she can't believe it*). I have something better than hope, I think!

Proctor. Abby, you'll put it out of mind. I'll not be comin' for you more.

Abigail. You're surely sportin' with me.

500 **Proctor.** You know me better.

Abigail. I know how you clutched my back behind your house and sweated like a stallion whenever I come near! Or did I dream that? It's she put me out, you cannot pretend it were you. I saw your face when she put me out, and you loved me then and you do now!

Proctor. Abby, that's a wild thing to say—

Abigail. A wild thing may say wild things. But not so wild, I think. I have seen you since she put me out; I have seen you nights.

Proctor. I have hardly stepped off my farm this sevenmonth.

Abigail. I have a sense for heat, John, and yours has drawn me to my window,
510 and I have seen you looking up, burning in your loneliness. Do you tell me you've never looked up at my window?

Proctor. I may have looked up.

Abigail (*now softening*). And you must. You are no wintry man. I *know* you, John. I know you. (*She is weeping.*) I cannot sleep for dreamin'; I cannot dream but I wake and walk about the house as though I'd find you comin' through some door.

(*She clutches him desperately*).

---

24. **◀ REREAD** Reread lines 460–523. What angers Abigail most about Proctor's refusal to see her? Why do you think she drank a charm to kill Goody Proctor?

_____

_____

_____

_____

_____

Proctor (*gently pressing her from him, with great sympathy but firmly*). Child—

520 **Abigail** (*with a flash of anger*). How do you call me child!

Proctor. Abby, I may think of you softly from time to time. But I will cut off my hand before I'll ever reach for you again. Wipe it out of mind. We never touched, Abby.

Abigail. Aye, but we did.

Proctor. Aye, but we did not.

Abigail (*with a bitter anger*). Oh, I marvel how such a strong man may let such a sickly wife be—

Proctor (*angered—at himself as well*). You'll speak nothin' of Elizabeth!

Abigail. She is blackening my name in the village! She is telling lies about me!

530 She is a cold, sniveling woman, and you bend to her! Let her turn you like a—

Proctor (*shaking her*). Do you look for whippin'?

(*A psalm is heard being sung below.*)

Abigail (*in tears*). I look for John Proctor that took me from my sleep and put

pretense: knowledge in my heart! I never knew what **pretense** Salem was, I never knew the lying lessons I was taught by all these Christian women and their covenanted[12] men! And now you bid me tear the light out of my eyes? I will not, I cannot! You loved me, John Proctor, and whatever sin it is, you love me yet!

(*He turns abruptly to go out. She rushes to him.*) John, pity me, pity me!

(*The words "going up to Jesus" are heard in the psalm, and* Betty *claps her ears*

540 *suddenly and whines loudly.*)

Abigail. Betty? (*She hurries to* Betty, *who is now sitting up and screaming.*

Proctor *goes to* Betty *as* Abigail *is trying to pull her hands down, calling* "Betty!")

unnerved: **Proctor** (*growing **unnerved***). What's she doing? Girl, what ails you? Stop that wailing!

---

[12]**covenanted:** In Puritan religious practice, the men of a congregation would make an agreement, or covenant, to govern the community and abide by its beliefs and practices.

---

25. **READD** ▶ As you read lines 524–573, continue to cite textual evidence.

- Underline details that show a change in Betty's condition.
- Circle details that describe the other characters' reactions.
- In the margin, explain what Mrs. Putnam thinks is happening to Betty.

> "She is blackening my name in the village! She is telling lies about me!"

(*The singing has stopped in the midst of this, and now* Parris *rushes in.*)

Parris. What happened? What are you doing to her? Betty! (*He rushes to the bed, crying,* "Betty, Betty!" Mrs. Putnam *enters, feverish with curiosity, and with her* Thomas Putnam *and* Mercy Lewis. Parris, *at the bed, keeps lightly slapping* 550 Betty*'s face, while she moans and tries to get up.*)

Abigail. She heard you singin' and suddenly she's up and screamin'.

Mrs. Putnam. The psalm! The psalm! She cannot bear to hear the Lord's name!

Parris. No. God forbid. Mercy, run to the doctor! Tell him what's happened here! (Mercy Lewis *rushes out.*)

Mrs. Putnam. Mark it for a sign, mark it!

(Rebecca Nurse, *seventy-two, enters. She is white-haired, leaning upon her walking-stick.*)

Putnam (*pointing at the whimpering* Betty). That is a notorious sign of 560 witchcraft afoot, Goody Nurse, a **prodigious** sign!

prodigious:

Mrs. Putnam. My mother told me that! When they cannot bear to hear the name of—

Parris (*trembling*). Rebecca, Rebecca, go to her, we're lost. She suddenly cannot bear to hear the Lord's—

(Giles Corey, *eighty-three, enters. He is knotted with muscle, canny, inquisitive, and still powerful.*)

26. **◄ REREAD** Reread lines 524–538. As Proctor responds to Abigail's insults about Elizabeth, what do his words and the stage directions suggest about his view of his marriage?

_____

_____

_____

Rebecca. There is hard sickness here, Giles Corey, so please to keep the quiet.

Giles. I've not said a word. No one here can testify I've said a word. Is she going to fly again? I hear she flies.

570   **Putnam.** Man, be quiet now!

(*Everything is quiet. Rebecca walks across the room to the bed. Gentleness exudes from her. Betty is quietly whimpering, eyes shut. Rebecca simply stands over the child, who gradually quiets.*)

SHORT RESPONSE

Cite Text Evidence   The plot of *The Crucible* slowly becomes more and more complicated. Why do you think Miller chooses to reveal information gradually rather than all at once? Look back at your reading notes and be sure to support your ideas by **citing evidence from the text.**

_____

_____

_____

_____

_____

_____

_____

_____

_____

_____

_____

_____

_____

_____

Background *Science is about collecting and interpreting data, while ethics is about the moral code with which we live our lives. The distinction is clear in Hume's Law, a philosophical theory that says we can't derive a moral judgment from mere assertions of facts. However, most people would agree that advances in science should be accompanied by the guidelines that ethics can provide. In the following essay,* **Freeman Dyson** *makes the case for ethics in scientific endeavors. Dyson is a famous physicist and mathematician who was born in England and became a United States citizen in 1957.*

Science, Guided by Ethics

Essay by Freeman Dyson

CLOSE READ
Notes

1. ▭ As you read lines 1–11, begin to collect and cite text evidence.

   - Circle the central idea in lines 1–6.
   - Underline definitions of green technology and gray technology in lines 1–6.
   - In the margin, explain how lines 7–11 use details to build support for Dyson's central idea.

May 29, 2000

Throughout history, people have used technology to change the world. Our technology has been of two kinds, green and gray. Green technology is seeds and plants, gardens and vineyards and orchards, domesticated horses and cows and pigs, milk and cheese, leather and wool. Gray technology is bronze and steel, spears and guns, coal and oil and electricity, automobiles and airplanes and rockets, telephones and computers.

Civilization began with green technology, with agriculture and animal-breeding, 10,000 years ago. Then, beginning about 3,000 years ago, gray technology became dominant, with mining and metallurgy and machinery.

10 For the last 500 years, gray technology has been racing ahead and has given birth to the modern world of cities and factories and supermarkets.

exploit:

The dominance of gray technology is coming to an end. During the last 50 years, we have achieved a fundamental understanding of the processes in living cells. With understanding comes the ability to **exploit** and control. Out of the knowledge acquired by modern biology, modern biotechnology[1] is growing. The new green technology will give us the power, using only sunlight as a source of energy, and air and water and soil as materials, to manufacture and recycle chemicals of all kinds.

20 Our gray technology of machines and computers will not disappear, but green technology will be moving ahead even faster. Green technology can be cleaner, more flexible and less wasteful than our existing chemical industries. A great variety of manufactured objects could be grown instead of made. Green technology could supply human needs with far less damage to the natural environment. And green technology could be a great equalizer, bringing wealth to the tropical areas, of the planet, which have most of the world's sunshine, people and poverty.

I am saying that green technology could do all these good things, not that green technology will do all these good things. To make these good things happen, we need not only the new technology but the political and economic 30 conditions that will give people all over the world a chance to use it.

_____

[1] **biotechnology:** the manipulation of living organisms or their components to produce useful products (such as pest resistant crops).

2. **◀ REREAD** Reread lines 1–11. Evaluate the content of these paragraphs. Is Dyson effective in making the facts clear?

_____

_____

_____

_____

3. **READ ▶** As you read lines 12–36, continue to cite textual evidence.

- Underline the claims Dyson makes about the benefits of green technology.
- In the margin, paraphrase Dyson's point of view.
- Circle the sentence that summarizes how Dyson thinks new green technology might be accomplished.

"

We all know that green technology has a dark side, just as gray technology has a dark side.

"

To make these things happen, we need a powerful push from ethics. We need a consensus of public opinion around the world that the existing gross inequalities in the distribution of wealth are intolerable. In reaching such a consensus, religions must play an essential role. Neither technology alone nor religion alone is powerful enough to bring social justice to human societies, but technology and religion working together might do the job.

We all know that green technology has a dark side, just as gray technology has a dark side. Gray technology brought us hydrogen bombs as well as telephones. Green technology brought us anthrax bombs as well as antibiotics.
40   Besides the dangers of biological weapons, green technology brings other dangers having nothing to do with weapons. The ultimate danger of green technology comes from its power to change the nature of human beings by the application of genetic engineering[2] to human **embryos**.

embryo:

---

[2] **genetic engineering:** the development and application of science and technology that allows direct manipulation of genes in order to change the hereditary traits of a cell, organism, or population.

---

4. **◄ REREAD**. Reread lines 31–36. How does Dyson define social justice? What does he say we need in order for green technology to become a "great equalizer?"

_____

_____

_____

_____

5. **READ ▶** As you read lines 37–58, continue to cite textual evidence.

• In the margin, note one danger of gray technology and one danger of green technology.

• Underline the summary statement Dyson makes in lines 51–58 about the possible benefits of biotechnology and of green technology.

• Circle the summary statement he makes in lines 51–58 about the possible evils of green technology.

If we allow a free market in human genes, wealthy parents will be able to buy what they consider superior genes for their babies. This could cause a splitting of humanity into hereditary castes. Within a few generations, the children of rich and poor could become separate species. Humanity would then have regressed all the way back to a society of masters and slaves. No matter how strongly we believe in the virtues of a free market economy, the free

50 market must not extend to human genes.

I see two tremendous goods coming from biotechnology: first, the alleviation of human misery through progress in medicine, and second, the transformation of the global economy through green technology spreading wealth more **equitably** around the world.

equitably:

6. REREAD Reread lines 37–50. What does Dyson say is the "ultimate danger" he sees in green technology? In what way does he support his claim? Support your answer with explicit textual evidence.

_____

_____

_____

_____

_____

> **Science and religion should work together to abolish the gross inequalities that prevail in the modern world.**

The two great evils to be avoided are the use of biological weapons and the corruption of human nature by buying and selling genes. I see no scientific reason why we should not achieve the good and avoid the evil. The obstacles to achieving the good are political rather than technical.

Unfortunately a large number of people in many countries are strongly
60 opposed to green technology, for reasons having little to do with the real dangers. It is important to treat the opponents with respect, to pay attention to their fears, to go gently into the new world of green technology so that neither human dignity nor religious conviction is violated. If we can go gently, we have a good chance of achieving within a hundred years the goals of ecological sustainability and social justice that green technology brings within our reach.

The great question for our time is how to make sure that the continuing scientific revolution brings benefits to everybody rather than widening the gap between rich and poor.

To lift up poor countries, and poor people in rich countries, from poverty,
70 technology is not enough. Technology must be guided and driven by ethics if it is to do more than provide new toys for the rich. Scientists and business leaders who care about social justice should join forces with environmental and religious organizations to give political clout to ethics.

---

7. **READD ▶** As you read lines 59–77, continue to cite textual evidence.

- Circle Dyson's recommendation for dealing with opponents of green technology.
- Underline what he sees as "the great question for our time."
- In the margin, summarize the position Dyson states in lines 74–77.

Science and religion should work together to abolish the gross inequalities that prevail in the modern world. That is my vision, and it is the same vision that inspired Francis Bacon[3] 400 years ago, when he prayed that through science God would "endow the human family with new mercies."

---

[3] **Francis Bacon:** a natural philosopher, scientist, judge, statesman, and writer, Bacon (1561–1626) pondered questions of ethics in his writing, even in his works of natural philosophy.

8. ◄ **REREAD**   Reread lines 59–77. What is Dyson's point of view about the future of green technology? Support your answer with explicit textual evidence.

_____

_____

_____

_____

_____

SHORT RESPONSE

Cite Text Evidence   Do you think Dyson offers a convincing argument that green technology must be guided by ethics? Review your reading notes, and evaluate the merit of his claim and evidence offered. **Cite textual evidence** in your response.

_____

_____

_____

_____

_____

_____

_____

_____

Acknowledgments

Excerpt from "Abigail Adams' Last Act of Defiance" by Woody Holton from *American History* Magazine, April 2010. Text copyright © 2010 by Woody Holton. Reprinted by permission of Weider History Group.

"Ambush" from *The Things They Carried* by Tim O'Brien. Text copyright © 1990 by Tim O'Brien. Reprinted by permission of Houghton Mifflin Harcourt Publishing Company, HarperCollins Publishers, Ltd. and Tim O'Brien.

"Bonding Over a Mascot" by Joe LaPointe from *The New York Times*, December 29, 2006, *www.nytimes.com*. Text copyright © 2006 by The New York Times Company. Reprinted by permission of PARS International, on behalf of The New York Times.

Excerpt from "Act 1" from *The Crucible* by Arthur Miller. Text copyright © 1952, 1953, 1954, renewed 1980, 1981, 1982 by Arthur Miller. Reprinted by permission of Viking Penguin, a division of Penguin Group (USA) Inc. and The Wylie Agency, Inc.

Excerpt from "The General History of Virginia" by John Smith from *The Complete Works on Captain John Smith, 1580-1631*, edited by Philip L. Barbour. Text copyright © 1986 by The University of North Carolina Press. Reprinted by permission of The University of North Carolina Press.

"Indian Boy Love Song (#2)" from *The Business of Fancydancing* by Sherman Alexie. Text copyright © 1992 by Sherman Alexie. Reprinted by permission of Hanging Loose Press.

"Mother Tongue" from *The Opposite of Fate* by Amy Tan. Text copyright © 1989 by Amy Tan. First appeared in Threepenny Review. Reprinted by permission of the Sandra Djikstra Literary Agency and the author.

"Ode to a Large Tuna in the Market" by Pablo Neruda, translated by Robin Robertson from *Poetry* Magazine. Text copyright © 2011 by the Fundacion Pablo Neruda. Reprinted by permission of the University of California Press and the Agencia Literaria Carmen Balcells.

Excerpt from "Reflection on the Atomic Bomb" by Gertrude Stein. Text copyright © 1946 by Gertrude Stein. Reprinted by permission of David Higham Associates Ltd.

"Science, Guided by Ethics, Can Lift Up the Poor" (Retitled: "Science, Guided by Ethics") by Freeman Dyson from *The New York Times*, May 29, 2000, www.nytimes.com. Text copyright © 2000 by The New York Times Company. Reprinted by permission of PARS International, on behalf of The New York Times.

"Spoiling Walden: Or How I Learned to Stop Worrying and Love Cape Wind" by David Gessner from *ONEARTH* Magazine, December 12, 2011, *www.onearth.com*. Text copyright © 2011 by David Gessner. Reprinted by permission of the National Resources Defense Council.

"The Weary Blues" from *The Collected Poems of Langston Hughes* by Langston Hughes, edited by Arnold Rampersad with David Roessel, Associate Editor. Text copyright © 1994 by the Estate of Langston Hughes. Reprinted by permission of Alfred A. Knopf, a division of Random House, Inc., and Harold Ober Associates, Inc. Any third party use of this material, outside of this publication, is prohibited. Interested parties must apply directly to Random House, Inc. for permission.

"The Yuckiest Food in the Amazon" by Mary Roach from *Salon*, December 15, 1998, *www.salon.com*. Text copyright © 2012 by Salon Media Group, Inc. Reprinted by permission of Salon Media Group, Inc.

Index of Titles & Authors